English Pronunciation for Communication

【Revised Edition】

コミュニケーションへの英語発音演習
【改訂新版】

杉森直樹　小泉節子　杉森幹彦

NAN'UN-DO

Download Audio

音声ファイル
無料 DL
のご案内

このテキストの音声を無料で視聴（ストリーミング）・ダウンロードできます。自習用音声としてご活用ください。
以下のサイトにアクセスしてテキスト番号で検索してください。

https://nanun-do.com　テキスト番号［ **512234** ］

※ 無線 LAN（WiFi）に接続してのご利用を推奨いたします。

※ 音声ダウンロードは Zip ファイルでの提供になります。
お使いの機器によっては別途ソフトウェア（アプリケーション）の導入が必要となります。

※ English Pronunciation for Communication <Revised Edition>
音声ダウンロードページは以下の QR コードからもご利用になれます。

Read by

Hannah Grace
Jennifer Skidmore
Chris Koprowski

English Pronunciation for Communication <Revised Edition>
コミュニケーションへの英語発音演習【改訂新版】

改訂新版はしがき

本書の初版は小泉節子先生と私の父である杉森幹彦の両氏によって執筆された。当時はまだインターネットも知られておらず、メディアもアナログ全盛の時代であった。このような時代であったにもかかわらず、メディア教材を用いて英語の発音を実践的かつ体系的に学ぶことを目指した本書が出版されたのは画期的なことであったと言える。発音教材としての本書の特徴は、ネイティブスピーカーが教科書の母音や子音を実際に発音する様子を収録したビデオテープが付属していることであった。今でこそネットの動画配信サイトで英語の発音に関するビデオを見ることは容易であるが、当時はこのような動画が付属した発音の教科書はほとんど無く、貴重なものであった。また、豊富な例文や演習問題に加え、Mother Goose や Nursery Rhyme で英語の発音をやさしく学べるようになっているのも本書の特徴である。このようなことから、本書は長年にわたって英語の発音演習や音声学の教科書として使用されてきたが、刊行から時が経ち、時代の変化に伴って改訂を行う必要が出てきた。そこで、初版のオリジナルコンテンツのよさを残しつつ、単語や例文、解説等について必要な部分の改訂を行った。改訂版ではレッスン構成や使用している発音記号等は初版のものを踏襲しているが、付属教材の音声とビデオを全面的に収録し直すと共に、教授用資料には確認テストとして利用できるリスニングの Review Quiz を追加した。

今回の改訂が実現できたのは、私が長年学会でお世話になっている千葉商科大学名誉教授の酒井志延先生のお陰である。先生から南雲堂を通じて打診を頂き、本書の改訂企画が具体化した。また、南雲堂の加藤敦氏には本書の改訂企画や編集について様々な面でお世話になった。お二人にはこの場を借りて感謝の意を表する次第である。

現代が多様な英語変種を認める EIL(English as an International Language) の時代であっても、その人の英語力を示す指標の一つとして発音の重要性は変わらない。本書に収録されている豊富なコンテンツを活用し、国際社会でも通じる英語の発音を効果的に身につけて頂ければ幸いである。本書が今後も英語の発音演習の教科書として多くの方々の学習に役立つことを願っている。

2023 年 10 月

改訂新版編著者

はしがき

本書は日本人の学生を対象に編集された英語発音演習の教本である。これは単なる理論的な音声学のテキストというよりも、実際のコミュニケーションに役立つ力を養成するためのテキストである。発音については、アメリカ英語とイギリス英語の違いを比較しながら、アメリカ英語の発音を基本としている。編集の基本方針は次の通りである。

1. 発音記号を正確にそして容易に覚えられるように、簡単で頻度の高い単語を用例として選んでいる。

2. 正しい発音の方法を系統的に学習し、正確で自然に発音できる力が養成されるように教材の内容と配列を工夫している。

3. 発音や聴き取り訓練が単調にならないように、学習形式に変化をもたせ、楽しい雰囲気の中で学習できるようにしている。例えば、Nursery Rhyme, Poem, Passageを豊富に取り入れている。特にNursery RhymeやMother Gooseは英語国民の言語感覚や生活感覚に染み込んだものであり、英語とこれらの伝承童謡とは切り離して考えることはできない。英語のリズムや文化や感情、即ち「英語の心」が自然に身体で覚えられるようできるだけ多く採用したので、これらを暗唱して口ずさむようにしてほしい。

本書の構成とその狙いは以下の通りであるので、その趣旨をよく理解して学習されることを望んでいる。

1. 第一章の母音と子音では、Words (1) として、個々の音素を含んだ基本語を列挙し、その音が単語のどこにあるかによって、Initial（語頭）、Medial（語中）、Final（語末）に分類されている。

2. Words (2) では英語の複雑なspellingと発音との関係がまとめられている。例えば、同じ [iː] の音でもkeyやmachine等のようにspellingが一定でないために日本人にとって発音しにくいものやhalfやknockのように現代英語では発音されない黙字が集められている。

3. 子音の部では、spring の spr- のように日本語の音韻構造では見られない子音結合と、実際のコミュニケーションで自然に話される場合に起こる音声変化—連結、同化、脱落—を整理し、聴き取りにくいポイントを要領よく練習できるようにまとめられている。

4. 母音、子音の個々の発音練習も基本的には必要であるが、実際の言語活動の場では、リズムとイントネーションが大切である。意味の違いをもたらすストレスや、文の種類、状況，心理状態、感情等によって微妙に変化するイントネーションにも重点が置かれているので、モデル音声をよく聞いて反復練習し、英語のリズムとイントネーションにも馴れ、英語を身体で覚えるようにしてほしい。

5. 英米の違いや日本語に無い発音の要領、音声学上の注意すべき要点等がKey Pointsとして随所にまとめられているので、それを手がかりとして更に深く学習してほしい。

このテキストには音声の他に、母音と子音の発音を録画した映像が用意されている。モデルの口や舌の動きをよく見て反復練習することによって、発音の要領をマスターすることができるであろう。

英語や英語音声学の授業が楽しい雰囲気の中で効果的に行われ、演習を通して実際のコミュニケーションに役立つ運用力が養成されることを期待している。

2023 年 10 月
著者
（初版はしがきより）

目次

Key Points 一覧表

Index of First Lines: Nursery Rhymes & Poems

発音器官 (Speech Organs)

Vocal Cords（声帯）の状態

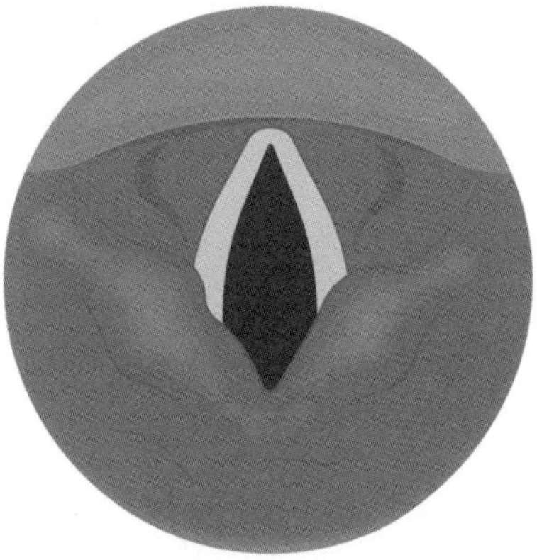

voiceless sound

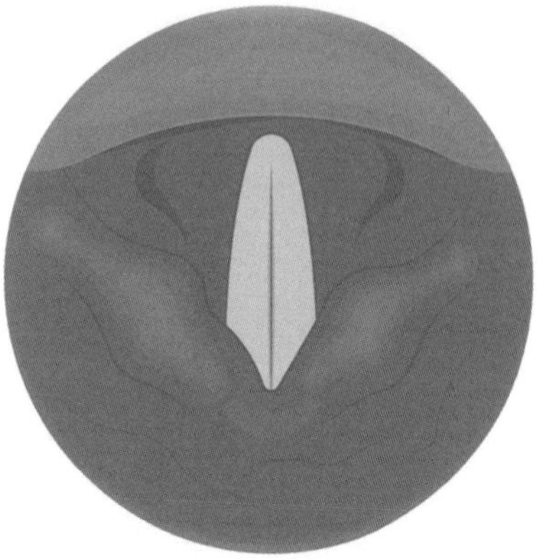

voiced sound

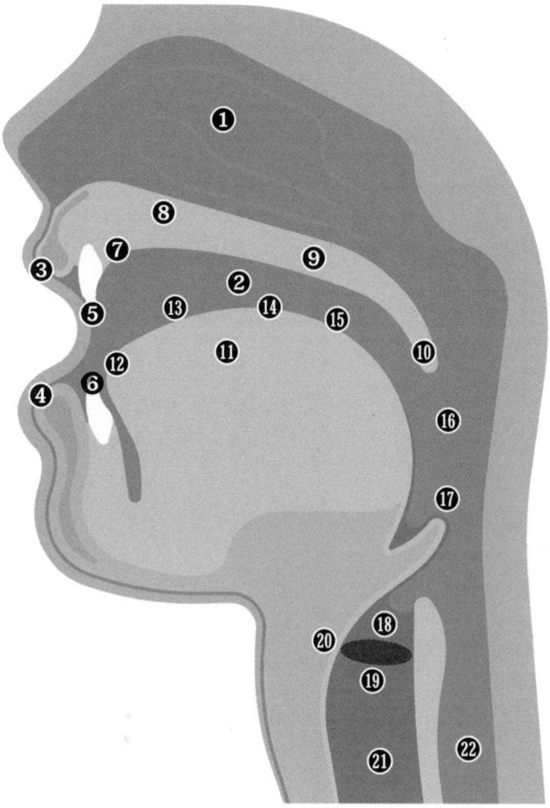

1. 鼻腔 (Nasal Cavity)
2. 口腔 (Oral Cavity)
3. 上唇 (Upper Lip)
4. 下唇 (Lower Lip)
5. 上歯 (Upper Teeth)
6. 下歯 (Lower Teeth)
7. 歯茎 (Teeth–ridge)
8. 硬口蓋 (Hard Palate)
9. 軟口蓋 (Soft Palate/Velum)
10. 口蓋垂 (Uvula)
11. 舌 (Tongue)
12. 舌先 (Tip of the Tongue)
13. 前舌面 (Front of the Tongue)
14. 中舌面 (Middle of the Tongue)
15. 後舌面 (Back of the Tongue)
16. 咽頭 (Pharynx)
17. 喉頭蓋 (Epiglottis)
18. 声門 (Glottis)
19. 声帯 (Vocal Cords)
20. 喉頭 (Larynx)
21. 気管 (Trachea)
22. 食道 (Gullet)

CHAPTER I

VOWELS & CONSONANTS

I. VOWELS & DIPHTHONGS

音声収録箇所は,Chapter I ～Chapter IIの練習，Exercises, Nursery Rhymes & Poems で,ヘッドフォンマーク（🎧）で示してあります。

英語の母音分類図表

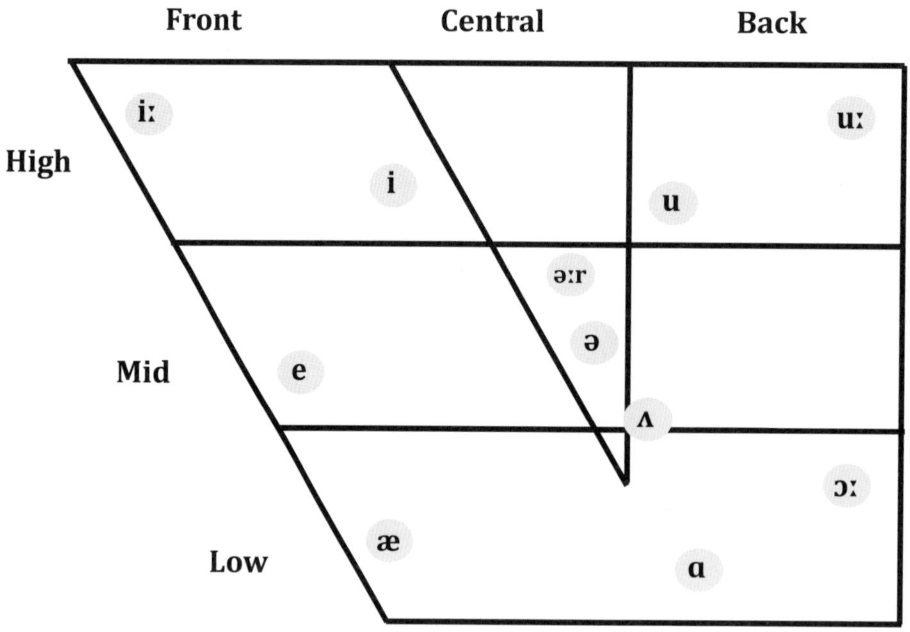

母音発音記号一覧表

English Vowels

	記号	例
1.	[iː]	eat
2.	[i]/[ɪ]	ink
3.	[e]	egg
4.	[æ]	act
5.	[ɑːr]	are
6.	[ɑ]	odd
7.	[ʌ]	up
8.	[ɔː]	all
9.	[uː]	cool
10.	[u]/[ʊ]	book
11.	[əːr] [ɚː]	earn
12.	[ər] [ɚ]	brother
13.	[ə]	about

English Diphthongs

	記号	例
1.	[ei]	aim
2.	[ai]	ice
3.	[au]	out
4.	[ɔi]	oil
5.	[ou]	oak
6.	[iər] [iɚ]	ear
7.	[ɛər] [ɛɚ]	air
8.	[ɔər] [ɔɚ]	oar
9.	[uər] [uɚ]	poor

Lesson 01

[iː]–[i]

1 [iː] (High Front Unrounded Vowel)

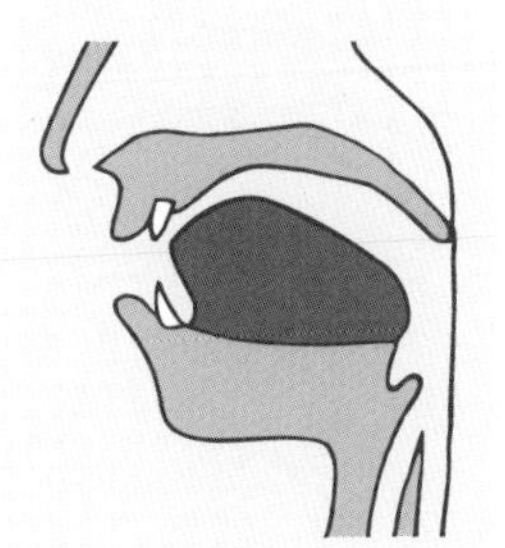

日本語［イー］と大体同じであるが唇をもっと緊張して横に張り下顎を後に引く。

A. Words (1)

Initial	Medial	Final
each	clean	pea
east	peace	sea
eel	green	me
evening	chief	bee
evil	receipt	ski

B. Words (2)

key, mosquito, machine, unique, antique

C. Sentences

1. Sheila seems to be feeling weak this evening.
2. Please feel free to eat these meat pies.
3. Peter is leaving for Tennessee this week.
4. Please keep your feet under your seat.
5. Peaches are good to eat in summer.
6. Jean is sleeping peacefully under the peach tree.
7. I happened to meet Stephen in the street.
8. Do you like your tea weak or strong?
9. Seeing is believing.《諺》（百聞は一見にしかず）

2 [i] (High Front Unrounded Vowel)

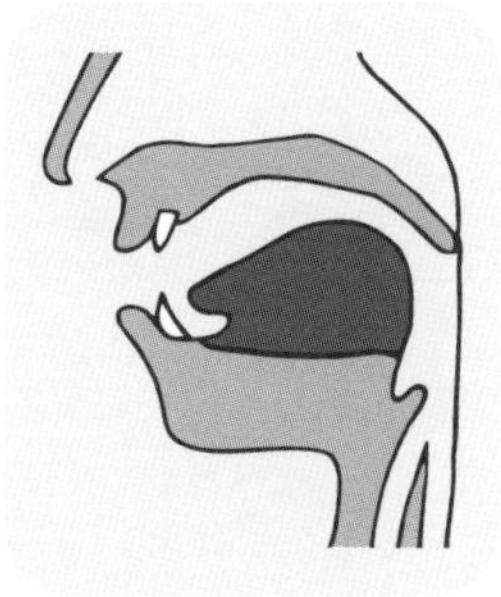

日本語の［エ］の形で［イ］と発音する。[iː] ほど唇を横に張らず緊張もゆるく，長さだけでなく音質的にちがっている。
＊ [ɪ] と表記される場合もある。

A. Words (1) 7

Initial	Medial	Final
image	big	NONE
infinite	exhibit	—
ink	script	—
instant	build	—
English	women	—

B. Words (2) 8

busy, edition, minute(*n.*), mischief, pretty, vineyard

C. Sentences 9

1. It's difficult for me to fill in the blanks on English quizzes.
2. Jim's little sister is pretty.
3. It's a pity Jill is still ill in bed.
4. Rick will quit the gym this December.
5. Monday, Tuesday and Wednesday are busy days for these women.

D. Compare the length of [i] in each pair. 10

1. bit—bid	3. hit—hid	5. mitt—mid
2. Dick—dig	4. lit—lid	6. pick—pig

3 Contrast between [iː] and [i]

A. Words 11

1. eat—it
2. eel—ill
3. feast—fist
4. feel—fill
5. heat—hit
6. lead—lid
7. leave—live
8. meat—mit
9. reach—rich
10. sheep—ship
11. scene—sin
12. sleep—slip

B. Sentences 12

1. I didn't buy it to eat.
2. List at least fifteen reasons.
3. Liz lives near Cricket Creek.
4. Either read the magazine or get rid of it.
5. The Queen's sister visited Greece and Egypt.
6. Jean's niece is still in Michigan, isn't she?
7. Please feel free to fill your dish.
8. Mickey is sitting in Minnie's seat.
9. The dean couldn't speak over the din.
10. Tim is going to leave his country to live here.

Nursery Rhymes 1 (Memorize) 13

(a)

I had a little hen,
The prettiest ever seen;
She washed up the dishes,
And kept the house clean.

(b)

Jack and Jill went up the hill
To fetch a pail of water.
Jack fell down and broke his crown
And Jill came tumbling after.

Exercise 1

A. Listen carefully and circle the letter of the words or sentences which are correctly pronounced.

14

1. a) did b) deed c) deed
2. a) dill b) deal c) dill
3. a) feet b) feet c) fit
4. a) leap b) lip c) leap
5. a) pick b) peak c) peak
6. a) I see a ship over there.
   b) I see a sheep over there.
   c) I see a ship over there.
7. a) Where did you sleep?
   b) Where did you slip?
   c) Where did you slip?
8. a) Try this mitt.
   b) Try this meat.
   c) Try this mitt.

B. Listen and fill in the blanks. 15

1. a. Let me (   ) the pitcher.
   b. Let me (   ) the pitcher.
2. a. The boy (   ) the dog.
   b. The boy (   ) the dog.
3. a. The word is not (   ).
   b. The word is not (   ).

Lesson 02

[e]–[ei]

1 [e] (Mid Front Unrounded Vowel)

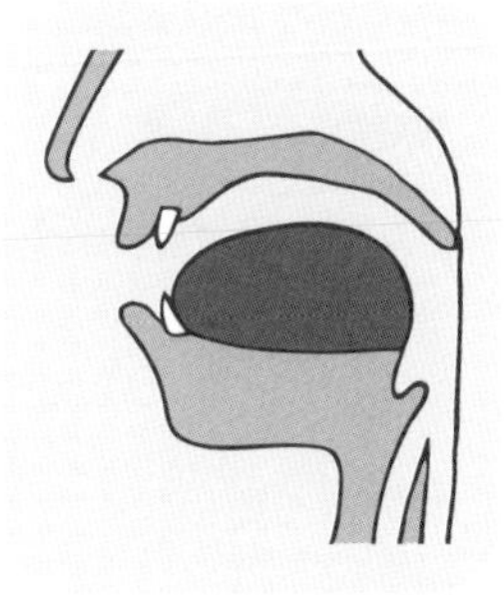

日本語の［エ］とほぼ同じであるが，
少し口を大きく開き，唇は横に張る。

A. Words (1) 16

Initial	Medial	Final
egg	bed	NONE
engine	breakfast	—
every	bury	—
any	friend	—
envelope	guest	—

B. Words (2) 17

lead(*n.*), leopard, measure, pleasure, said, says, sweat, weapon

C. Sentences 18

1. Ted is very clever. He will enter an excellent college—Cambridge, they say.
2. Yesterday Jenny read the text very well, and she was best in the test.
3. Helen was never at her desk, I guess.
4. The guest says she didn't bring her sweater.
5. In the entrance exams, everybody brought several extra pencils.

D. Compare the length of [e] in each pair. 19

1. bet—bed	3. let—led	5. set—said
2. debt—dead	4. peck—peg	6. wet—wed

2 [ei] (Diphthong)

日本語の［エ］よりも口を横にひらき，舌を緊張させて強く［ e ］と発音し，そのあとに軽く［ i ］をそえる。二音節とならないように全体を一音節として発音する。

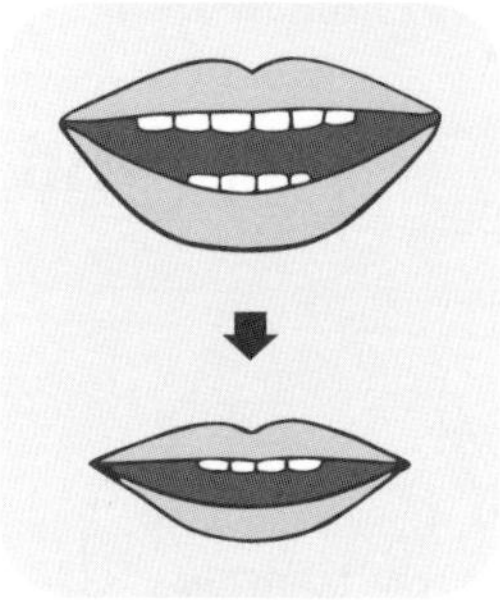

A. Words (1) 20

Initial	Medial	Final
aim	bake	bay
age	rain	they
ache	neighbor	sleigh
ancient	became	weigh
eight	bass	yea

B. Words (2) 21

gauge, jail, ballet, champaign, champagne

C. Sentences 22

1. Take the baby to bed at eight.
2. Haste makes waste.《諺》(急がば回れ)
3. They say it rained heavily on their wedding day.
4. Let's play baseball later today.
5. They will stay at the place and enjoy the change of the air until April.
6. Waiter, please bring me a rare steak and a baked potato.
7. It's O.K. to make mistakes.
8. The rain in Spain stays mainly in the plain! (*My Fair Lady*)

3 Contrast between [e] and [ei]

A. Words (1) 23

1. bet—bait
2. debt—date
3. edge—age
4. get—gate
5. fell—fail
6. let—late
7. met—mate
8. pen—pain
9. sell—sail
10. test—taste
11. wet—wait, weight
12. tell—tale

B. Sentences 24

1. You may get wet if you wait.
2. There was a gate to get through.
3. Tell us some amazing tales, please.
4. 'Breakfast' means to 'break' 'fast.' That is, you fast during the night and break it in the morning. That's why 'breakfast' is the first meal of the day.
5. Better late than never. 《諺》（遅くともしないよりはまし）

4 Cumulative Contrast [iː]–[i]–[e]–[ei]

25

1. beat—bit—bet—bate
2. feel—fill—fell—fail
3. heal—hill—hell—hail
4. liter—litter—letter—later
5. meat—mitt—met—mate
6. peel—pill—pell—pale
7. peen—pin—pen—pain
8. seal—sill—sell—sail

(a) Rain, rain, go away,
Come again another day,
Little Johnny wants to play.

(b) Rain, rain, go to Spain,
Never show your face again.

(c) Rain on the green grass,
And rain on the tree,
Rain on the house-top,
But not on me.

(d) If all the seas were one sea,
What a great sea that would be!
If all the trees were one tree,
What a great tree that would be!
And if all the axes were one axe,
What a great axe that would be!
And if all the men were one man,
What a great man that would be!
And if the great man took the great axe,
And cut down the great tree,
And let it fall into the great sea,
What a splish-splash that would be!

Exercise 2

A. Listen carefully and circle the letter of the words which are correctly pronounced.

1. a) let　　b) late　　c) let　　27
2. a) wren　　b) rain　　c) rain
3. a) fade　　b) fed　　c) fade
4. a) main　　b) main　　c) men
5. a) wait　　b) wet　　c) wet

B. Listen and fill in each blank with phonetic symbol [e] or [ei]. Then write the word in (　　　　).

28

1. a) Who could have [l　　　d] the boy there?　(　　　　)
   b) Who could have [l　　　d] the boy there?　(　　　　)
   c) Who could have [l　　　d] the boy there?　(　　　　)
2. a) I'll never forget the [d　　　t].　(　　　　)
   b) I'll never forget the [d　　　t].　(　　　　)
   c) I'll never forget the [d　　　t].　(　　　　)
3. a) The [r　　　n] is descending gently from the clouds.　(　　　　)
   b) The [r　　　n] is descending gently from the clouds.　(　　　　)
   c) The [r　　　n] is descending gently from the clouds.　(　　　　)
4. a) A great many daffodils grow in the [d　　　l].　(　　　　)
   b) A great many daffodils grow in the [d　　　l].　(　　　　)
   c) A great many daffodils grow in the [d　　　l].　(　　　　)
5. a) Do you like this [t　　　st]?　(　　　　)
   b) Do you like this [t　　　st]?　(　　　　)
   c) Do you like this [t　　　st]?　(　　　　)

Lesson 03

[æ]

[æ] (Low Front Unrounded Vowel)

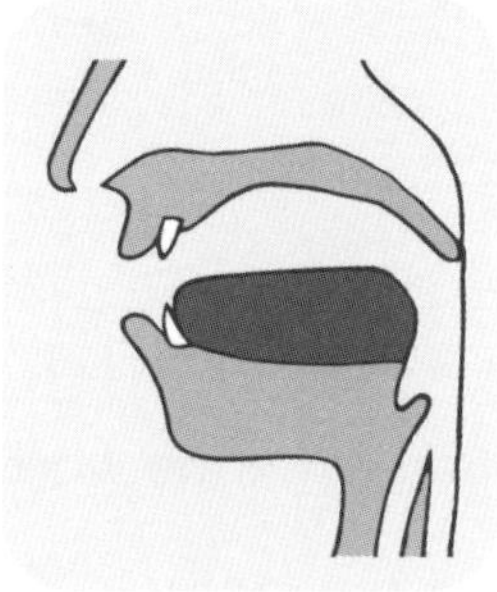

日本語の［エ］と［ア］の中間音。［ア］の口の形で［エ］と発音する。口を横方向にしっかりと引き、舌先を下歯に付けて少し長めに発音する。

A. Words (1) 29

Initial	Medial	Final
act	bat	NONE
apple	hand	—
atlas	Japan	—
atom	pageant	—
Africa	taxi	—

B. Words (2) 30

plaid, half, laugh, salmon, family, began

C. Sentences 31

1. Brad, did you see a black cat on Halloween?
2. It's too bad that Sally and Maggie have no camera.
3. Ann sang about a castle in a happy land.
4. Kathy has candy and apples in her basket.
5. Uncle Sam was panting as he ran with a heavy bag in his hand.
6. He who laughs last laughs best.《諺》（早まって喜ぶな）

Key Points 1 32-33

次の単語の下線部は，英語では [ɑː] [ɑ]，米語では一般に [æ] と発音されている。

after, bath, bathroom, brass, castle, cast, chance, class, classroom, can't, dance, fast, half, last, past, rather, task, vast

D. Compare the length of [æ] in each pair. 34

1. bat—bad
2. back—bag
3. hat—had
4. mat—mad
5. pat—pad
6. sat—sad

E. Contrast between [æ] and [e]. 35

1. bad—bed
2. bag—beg
3. band—bend
4. dad—dead
5. gas—guess
6. had—head
7. ham—hem
8. latter—letter
9. man—men
10. pan—pen
11. pat—pet
12. sad—said

Nursery Rhymes 3 36

(a) Pat-a-cake, pat-a-cake, baker's man,
Bake me a cake as fast as you can.
Pat it and prick it, and mark it with B,
Put it in the oven for Baby and me.

(b) Jack Sprat could eat no fat,
His wife could eat no lean;
And so between them both, you see,
They licked the platter clean.

F. Passage for Reading (1) 37

Read the following story paying special attention to [æ], [e] and [ei].

Everyone knows that dogs follow their prey using their sense of smell. Dolphins have a special built-in sonar system to help them locate fish for food. Other animals use their keen vision or hearing. But how seals track their prey had been something of a mystery among zoologists; seals are able to hunt even in dark, cloudy waters, where their eyes and ears are ineffective.

But a team of German scientists has solved the mystery. It is the seals' whiskers that enable them to home in on the fish they eat. The hairs contain about 25,000 sensors. These can detect tiny vibrations in the water up to 180 meters away. The scientists believe that other mammals, including sperm whales, may use their whiskers to hunt with, too.

Exercise 3

A. Listen carefully and circle the letter of the words which are correctly pronounced.

38

1. a) cattle b) kettle c) cattle
2. a) last b) last c) lest
3. a) mat b) mat c) met
4. a) mess b) mass c) mass
5. a) sand b) send c) sand

B. Listen and fill in the blanks. 39

1. The hen (   ) where he (   ) her.
2. She (   ) she was (   ).
3. They (   ) money to buy (   ).
4. My bad (   ) made me (   ) behind.
5. It's not wise to (   ) a lion. It's not wise to (   ) one, either.
6. My sister is very proud of her (   ) shoes. I'm proud of my (   ) shoes.
7. This (   ) leaks. So does this (   ).
8. The (   ) brought a (   ).
9. The traffic was a (   ). There was a tangled (   ) of cars.
10. (   ) is the (   ) medicine. 《諺》（笑いは最良のくすり）

Lesson 04

[ɑːr]

1 [ɑːr] (Low Back Unrounded Vowel)

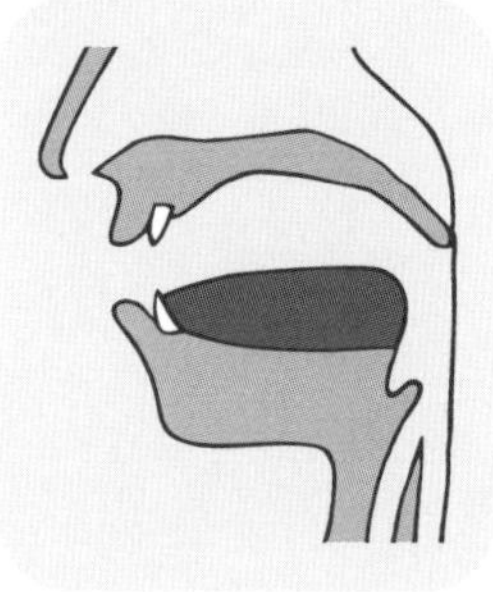

日本語の［アー］よりも口を大きく開いて発音し，最後に舌の先を少し後方にそらせてrの響きをそえる。イギリス英語ではこの[r]は発音されない。

A. Words 40-41

Initial	Medial	Final
are	carp	bar
arch	charge	car
argue	farther	far
arm	garden	jar
art	heart	star

B. Words (2) 42-43

bazaar, sergeant, memoir, sorry, tomorrow

C. Sentences 44-45

1. Marshal started to read the artist's article in front of the hearth.
2. Farmer Clark has a large barn full of artichokes.
3. Who's in charge of the garden party?
4. Marcy found a bargain at the art sale.
5. Barbara wants to be an architect or an artist.
6. Charlie could hardly park his car.

Nursery Rhymes 4

46-47

The Queen of Hearts
She made some tarts,
All on a summer's day;
The Knave of Hearts
He stole the tarts,
And took them clean away.

The King of Hearts
Called for the tarts,
And beat the knave full score;
The Knave of Hearts
Brought back the tarts,
And vowed he'd steal no more.

Exercise 4

A. Listen and write A for [æ] and B for [aːr] for each stressed vowel. 48

1. hearth ( )
2. happen ( )
3. apple ( )
4. arbor ( )
5. fat ( )
6. black ( )
7. practice ( )
8. garden ( )
9. atlas ( )
10. Africa ( )
11. rather ( )
12. alarm ( )
13. family ( )
14. arch ( )

B. Listen and circle the number of the word that is different from the others in each group. 49

1. (1) (2) (3)
2. (1) (2) (3)
3. (1) (2) (3)
4. (1) (2) (3)
5. (1) (2) (3)
6. (1) (2) (3)
7. (1) (2) (3)
8. (1) (2) (3)
9. (1) (2) (3)
10. (1) (2) (3)

Lesson 05 [ɑ]

[ɑ] (Low Back Unrounded Vowel)

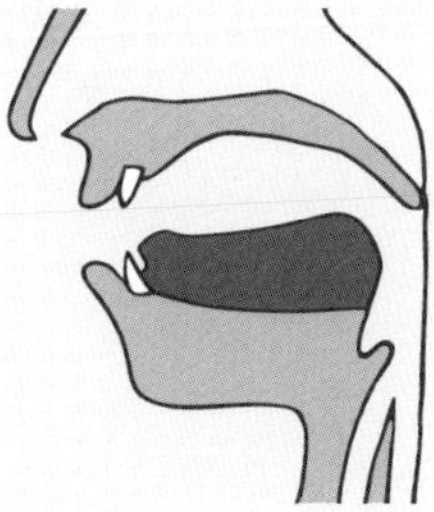

日本語の［ア］よりも口を大きくあけて，のどの奥の方から［ア］と発音する。長めに発音すると英語らしくなる。

A. Words (1) 50

Initial	Medial	Final
odd	top	NONE
occupy	model	—
olive	hot	—
opposite	rock	—
operator	bottom	—

B. Words (2) 51

honor, knowledge, John, yacht

Key Points 2 52-53

次の単語の下線部はイギリス英語では [ɔ], アメリカ英語では一般に [ɑ] と発音されている。

blond, body, box, clock, collar, concert, cotton, cooperate, doctor, doll, dollar, follow, god, honor, mom, modern, not, non-stop, quality, quantity, rob, shop, shot, stocking, watch

ただし，次の単語の下線部の場合は米語では一般に [ɔ]（[ɔː]）と発音され，[ɑ] となることは殆どない。

cloth, dog, long, loss, lost, soft, toss

C. Sentences 54

1. John and Bob wanted some hotdogs.
2. Yesterday, Molly forgot to put on her watch.
3. Donna and Scott flew non-stop to Chicago.
4. Holly wants me to watch for the doctor's yacht.
5. Tom's mom went holiday shopping.
6. She bought a pocket watch, a doll, a box of socks, a bottle of Scotch and two tickets to a rock concert.
7. Ron got a job as a top model.
8. Dr. Hopkins stopped Connie in the hospital lobby.
9. That blond is a topnotch photographer.
10. A watched pot never boils. 《諺》（待つ身は長い）

Nursery Rhymes 5 55

Hickory, dickory, dock,
The mouse ran up the clock,
**　The clock struck one,**
**　The mouse ran down,**
Hickory, dickory, dock.

D. Contrast between [æ] and [ɑ]. 56

1. add—odd
2. band—bond
3. bat—bot
4. cap—cop
5. cat—cot
6. Dan—Don
7. hat—hot
8. lack—lock
9. map—mop
10. pat—pot

Exercise 5

A. Listen carefully and circle the letter of the words or sentences which are correctly pronounced. 57

1. a) cap b) cop c) cop
2. a) Dan b) Dan c) Don
3. a) lock b) lock c) lack
4. a) mop b) map c) map
5. a) pat b) pat c) pot
6. a) Would you call it a cat?
   b) Would you call it a cot?
   c) Would you call it a cot?
7. a) I had a shack in the woods.
   b) I had a shock in the woods.
   c) I had a shock in the woods.
8. a) The map was hanging there.
   b) The mop was hanging there.
   c) The mop was hanging there.

B. Listen and fill in the blanks. 58

1. A ( ) cat ( ) my way.
2. You'll be ( ) without a ( ).
3. This ( ) is not advertised in ( ) magazines.
4. Our kitchen is full of ( ) and ( ).
5. ( ) put his straw ( ) on the ( ).

Lesson 06

[ʌ]

[ʌ] (Low Back Unrounded Vowel)

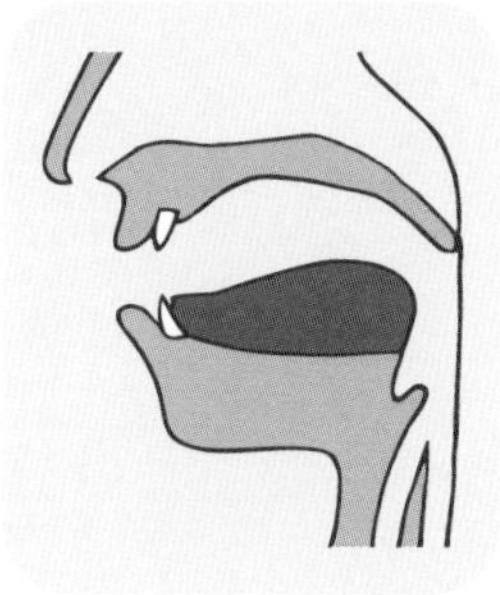

日本語の［ア］に［オ］を少し加味した音。口の奥で短く［ア］と発音する。

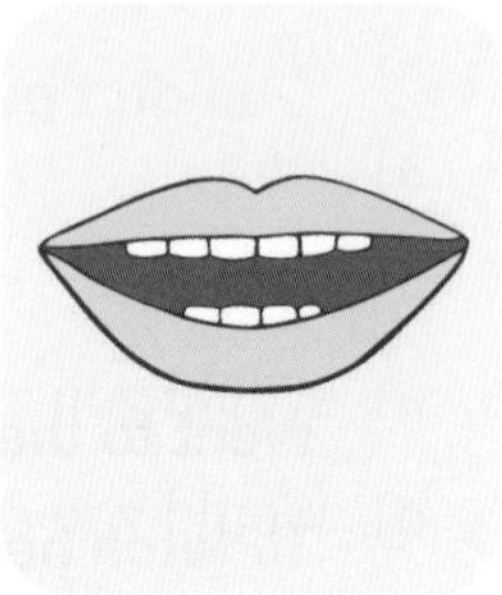

A. Words (1) 59

Initial	Medial	Final
other	duck	NONE
oven	London	—
up	love	—
under	nothing	—
ugly	country	—

B. Words (2) 60

blood, southern, does, what

C. Sentences 61

1. Last summer, my younger son read *Alice in Wonderland*.
2. Let's have lunch in the country some sunny day.
3. The other runner was lucky and won the cup.
4. Uncle Gus gets angry when he is hungry.
5. Learn to walk before you run. 《諺》（ころばぬ先の杖）
6. The Sunday puzzle is a tough one.
7. Uncle Judd loves buttered buns.
8. Rusty is unlucky in love.
9. Chuck missed the bus to Columbus.
10. Sully comes from the suburbs.

Nursery Rhymes 6 62

(a) Humpty Dumpty sat on a wall,
Humpty Dumpty had a great fall;
All the King's horses and all the King's men
Couldn't put Humpty together again.

(b) Old Mother Hubbard
Went to the cupboard
To fetch her poor dog a bone;
But when she came there
The cupboard was bare
And so the poor dog had none.

(c) Little Tommy Tucker
Sings for his supper,
What shall we give him?
White bread and butter.

D. Contrast between [ɑ] and [ʌ] 63

1. collar—color
2. cot—cut
3. chock—chuck
4. doll—dull
5. hot—hut
6. lock—luck
7. not—nut
8. poppy—puppy
9. robber—rubber
10. shock—shuck
11. shot—shut
12. sock—suck

E. Passage for Reading (2)

Read the following story paying special attention to [ɑ] and [ʌ]. 64

It was Tommy's birthday, and he was five years old. He got quite a lot of nice birthday presents from his family, and one of them was a beautiful big drum.

'Who gave him that thing?' Tommy's father said when he saw it.

'His grandfather did,' answered Tommy's mother.

'Oh,' said his father.

Of course, Tommy liked his drum very much. He made a terrible noise with it, but his mother didn't mind. His father was working during the day, and Tommy was in bed when he got home in the evening, so he didn't hear the noise.

But one of the neighbors didn't like the noise at all, so one morning a few days later, she took a sharp knife and went to Tommy's house while he was hitting his drum. She said to him, 'Hello, Tommy. You know, there's something very nice inside your drum. Here's a knife. Open the drum and let's find it.'

(Adapted from *Elementary Stories for Reproduction 2* by L.A. Hill)

Exercise 6

A. Listen to the audio and fill in the blanks. 65

1. The ( ) are swimming around the ( ).
2. He heard a ( ) and ( ) the door.
3. Ouch! This ( ) is too ( ) to pick up.
4. Wanda wore her ( ) ( ) to the test.
5. The ( ) stole her ( ) boots.
6. Look at the ( ) running around the red ( ).
7. Polly ( ) dogs. She has a ( ) and one ( ).

B. Listen and complete the following words. 66

1. co ___ ___ r
2. d ___ ___ l
3. s ___ ___ ck
4. d ___ ck
5. s ___ ___ thern
6. bl ___ ___ d
7. ch ___ ck
8. d ___ g
9. l ___ ck
10. sh ___ ___ ___ lec ___ ck

C. Listen and circle the number of the word that is different from the others in each group. 67

1. (1) (2) (3)
2. (1) (2) (3)
3. (1) (2) (3)
4. (1) (2) (3)
5. (1) (2) (3)
6. (1) (2) (3)
7. (1) (2) (3)
8. (1) (2) (3)
9. (1) (2) (3)
10. (1) (2) (3)

Lesson 07

[ɔː]–[ou]

1 [ɔː] (Low Back Rounded Vowel)

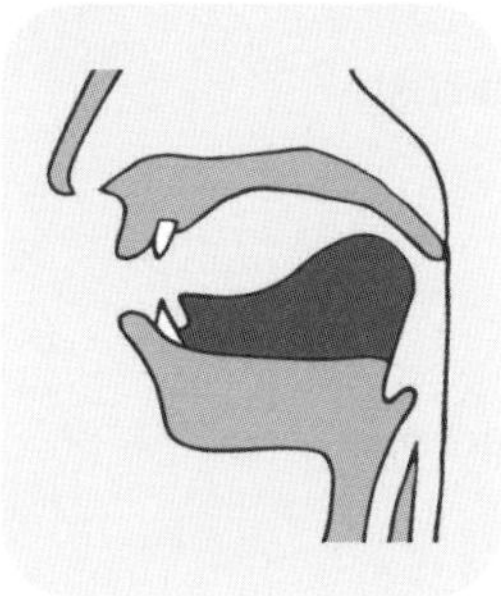

日本語の［オー］よりも口の開きが大きく，唇を突き出すようにしてまるめ，口の奥の方から［アー］と声を出す。

A. Words (1) 68

Initial	Medial	Final
all	ball	draw
author	cause	law
awful	dog	raw
office	cough	saw
often	lawn	thaw

B. Words (2) 69

abroad, broad, chalk, fog, golf, long, moss, talk, Maugham [mɔːm]（人名）

C. Sentences 70

1. Audrey went to Austria with her daughter.
2. Sean woke at dawn and mowed the lawn.
3. Paul taught students from Hong Kong in August.
4. The audience applauded Claudia's talk on the author.
5. A tall golfer teed off before a large audience in Palm Springs.

Poem 1 71

The black cat yawns,
Opens her jaws,
Stretches her legs,
And shows her claws.
Then she gets up
And stands on four
Long stiff legs
And yawns some more. (M. B. Miller)

2 [ou] (Diphthong)

日本語の［オ］よりも，少し唇をまるく突き出して，［ o ］と強く発音したのちに，軽く［ u ］をそえて［オゥ］と発音する。［ ɔː ］と［ ou ］とを明瞭に区別して発音することが大切である。

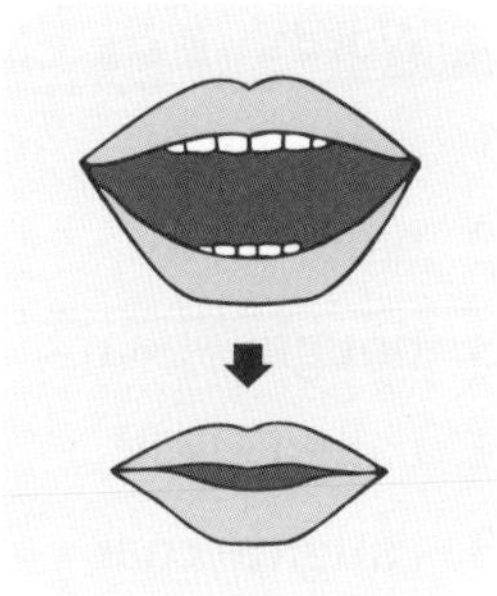

A. Words (1) 72

Initial	Medial	Final
oak	both	go
old	brooch	low
only	coat	sew
open	folk	though
own	post	toe

B. Words (2) 73

bureau, cocoa, oh, Holmes [houmz]（人名）, Seoul [soul]（地名）

C. Sentences 74

1. Old Joe spoke in a low voice.
2. A rolling stone gathers no moss. 《諺》（転石苔むさず）
3. They don't want to postpone their trip to Seoul.
4. I know Joan wrote this poem at home.
5. He's told that old joke over and over on the radio.

Nursery Rhymes 7 75

Pease porridge hot,
Pease porridge cold,
Pease porridge in the pot
Nine days old.

Some like it hot,
Some like it cold,
Some like it in the pot
Nine days old.

3 Contrast between [ɔː] and [ou]

A. Words 76

1. awe—owe
2. bald—bold
3. bought—boat
4. called—cold
5. caught—coat
6. law—low
7. lawn—loan
8. hall—hole
9. pause—pose
10. raw—row
11. taught—tote
12. walk—woke

B. Sentences 77

1. When I woke, I took a walk.
2. Every boy brought his own bowling ball.
3. I saw Dawn sew her coat.
4. Joan ought to go to the coast again this fall.
5. Joe's bought a boat but doesn't know how to row.
6. The poor old man almost always caught cold.
7. The law student was speaking in a low voice.
8. Paula taught Sophie how to play lawn tennis.
9. People who live in glass houses shouldn't throw stones.
   《諺》（弱点のある者は他人を批評非難せぬがよい）
10. All that glitters is not gold. 《諺》（輝くものすべてが金とはかぎらない）

C. Conversation 78

A: Hello. Holmes speaking.

B: Hello. This is Rose Hall. May I speak to Ms. Holmes?

A: I'm sorry, but she's talking on another phone. Would you like to wait, or should I have her call you back?

B: Oh, I'll call her again later.

Poems and Nursery Rhyme 2 79

THE TWENTY-FOURTH OF DECEMBER

The clock ticks slowly, slowly in the hall.
And slower and more slow the long hours crawl;
It seems as though today
Would never pass away;
The clock ticks slowly, s-l-o-w-l-y in the hall.

CARPENTERS

Saw, saw, saw away,
Saw the boards and saw the timbers.
Saw, saw, saw away,
We will build a house today.

Jerry Hall

Jerry Hall,
He is so small,
A rat could eat him,
Hat and all.

Exercise 7

A. Listen carefully and circle the letter of the words or sentences which are correctly pronounced.

1. a) call b) coal c) coal 80
2. a) fall b) foal c) fall
3. a) loan b) loan c) lawn
4. a) low b) law c) law
5. a) saw b) so c) saw
6. a) We found a big hole at the corner.
   b) We found a big hall at the corner.
   c) We found a big hole at the corner.
7. a) Look at that ball.
   b) Look at that bowl.
   c) Look at that ball.
8. a) She paused while walking.
   b) She posed while walking.
   c) She paused while walking.

B. Listen and fill in the blanks 81

1. a. Look at the (   ).
   b. Look at the (   ).
2. a. Let me help you with the (   ).
   b. Let me help you with the (   ).
3. a. The speaker (   ) everyone there.
   b. The speaker (   ) everyone there.

Lesson 08 [uː]–[u]

1 [uː] (High Back Rounded Vowel)

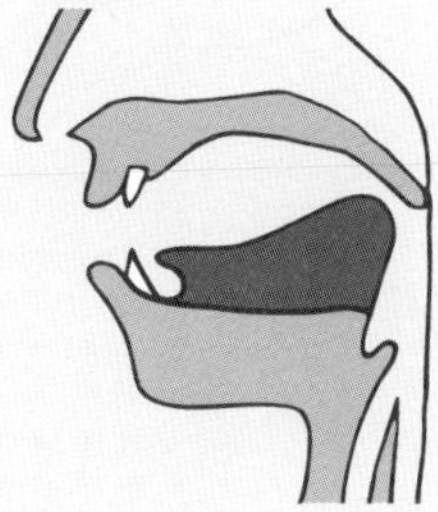

日本語の［ウー］よりも唇をまるめて前に突き出し，口笛を吹くときの口のかまえで長めに強く［ウー］と発音する。

A. Words (1) 82

Initial	Medial	Final
oodles	cool	blue
oolong	fruit	do
oops	move	new
ooze	rule	shoe
oozing	suit	you

B. Words (2) 83

recruit, rheumatism, queue, tomb, through, too

C. Sentences 84

1. Luke is moving to New Hampshire very soon.
2. Don't lose your loose-leaf notebook on the way to school.
3. Ruth and Lucy went to the zoo on a school tour.
4. Sue might choose a blue suit and blue boots.
5. It's nice to swim in the pool on cool evenings.

Nursery Rhyme & Poem 8 85

(a) I see the moon,
And the moon sees me;
God bless the moon,
And God bless me.

(b) Love the beautiful
Seek out the true,
Wish for the good
And the best do!

2 [u] (High Back Rounded Vowel)

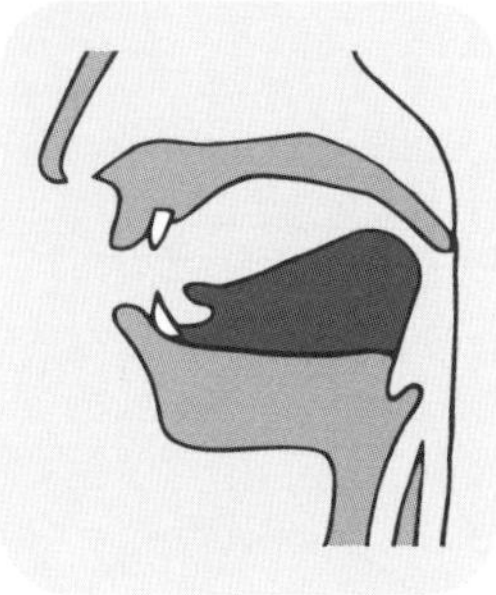

日本語の［ウ］よりも唇をまるめて前に突き出し，短く［ウ］と発音 する。［ウ］と［オ］の中間音の感 じ。[uː]とは音質的にちがっている。

＊[ʊ]と表記される場合もある。

A. Words (1) 86

Initial	Medial	Final
NONE	book	NONE
—	good	—
—	pull	—
—	should	—
—	wolf	—

B. Words (2) 87

bosom, could, look, put, woman, wool, would

C. Sentences 88

1. Little Red Riding Hood met a wolf in the woods.
2. Could you look up Woody's number in the address book?
3. You shouldn't push the door. Pull it!
4. Would you like to try the cook's fruit pudding?
5. Brooke is wearing a good-looking wool scarf.
6. That bully took my sugar cookies!

Nursery Rhyme 9 89

Pussy cat, pussy cat, where have you been?
I've been to London to look at the queen.
Pussy cat, pussy cat, what did you there?
I frightened a little mouse under her chair.

3 Contrast between [uː] and [u]

A. Words 90

1. cooed—could
2. fool—full
3. Luke—look
4. pool—pull
5. who'd—hood
6. wooed—would

B. Sentences 91

1. He stood up behind the stool.
2. The woman wouldn't look at the tombstone.
3. Lucy put her boots and shoes in my room.
4. Luke could see the full moon through the woods.
5. Who's that woman in the good-looking wool suit?
6. The proof of the pudding is in the eating. 《諺》（論より証拠）
7. No news is good news. 《諺》（便りのないのは良い便り）
8. Too many cooks spoil the stew. 《諺》（船頭多くして船山に上がる）

C. Conversation 92

A: What are you looking for, Ruth?

B: I'm looking for my cookbook. I thought I left it behind in this room.

A: I don't think I saw any cookbook when I came in.

B: I'm going to cook beef stew and bake some sugar cookies. That book has good recipes and I don't want to lose it.

Exercise 8

A. Listen carefully and circle the letter of the words which are correctly pronounced. 93

1.	a) full	b) full	c) fool
2.	a) hood	b) who'd	c) hood
3.	a) look	b) Luke	c) look
4.	a) pull	b) pool	c) pool
5.	a) should	b) shooed	c) should
6.	a) would	b) would	c) wooed

B. Listen and fill in the blanks. 94

1. They made a (   ) for the (   ).
2. The baby has a (   ) new (   ).
3. She just (   ) and (   ) at her (   ).
4. (   ) it be better to wait till (   )?
5. Don't (   ) my leg in the (   )!
6. It was so (   ) of me to eat that much (   ).
   I'm so (   ) now.

C. Listen and complete the following words. 95

1. l __ __ se
2. gr __ __ p
3. b __ __ om
4. w __ __ f
5. w __ __ __ en
6. tr __ th
7. b __ __ l
8. fr __ __ t
9. bu __ __ __ t
10. w __ __ n
11. r __ mor
12. thr __ __ __ __ / thr __ __
13. c __ __ l
14. h __ __ k

Lesson 09 [ə]–[ər]–[əːr]

1 [ə] (Mid Central Unrounded Vowel; Obscure Vowel; Neutral Vowel)

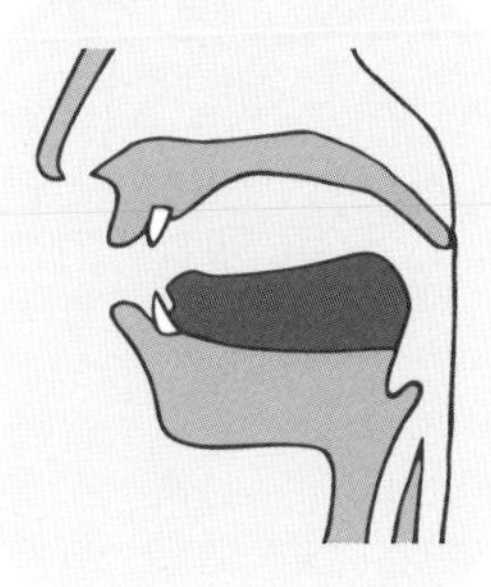

口を自然に少し開き，唇や舌の力をぬいて弱く［ア］と発音する。この音は［あいまい母音］（schwa）とも呼ばれる。

A. Words (1) 96

Initial	Medial	Final
about	company	camera
above	cruel	cinema
across	famous	opera
o'clock	police	sofa
offend	welcome	umbrella

B. Words (2) 97

parliament, today, tortoise

C. Sentences 98

1. My little brother spends about a thousand yen a week.
2. How about another cup of coffee? With a couple of cubes of sugar?
3. He is always on time. He arrived at the place right at one o'clock.
4. My father went up the hill alone with an umbrella.
5. After supper, Victor fell asleep on the sofa.

This [ə] (schwa) is used for any vowel or diphthong in an unstressed position.

（弱形と強形の項参照）

[ɚ] および [ɚː] は，英音 [ə] および [əː] に対応する米音。

[ɚː] は，[əː] 音に [r] を響かせた音。

2 [ər] ([ɚ]) (Mid Central Unrounded Vowel)

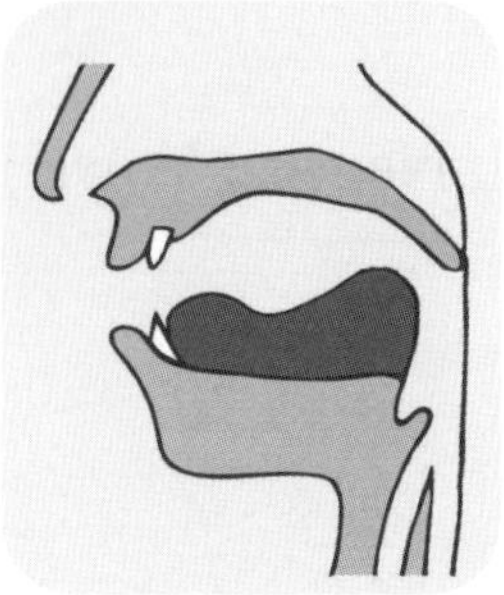

口を自然に少し開き，唇や舌の力をぬいて弱く［ア］と発音し，［ r ］の響きの音にする。イギリス英語ではこの［ r ］は発音されない。

A. Words (1) 99-100

Initial	Medial	Final
NONE	afternoon	brother
—	butterfly	dinner
—	entertain	doctor
—	interfere	sister
—	wonderful	teacher

B. Words (2) 101-102

cocker spaniel, fire fighter, beginner, kangaroo

C. Sentences 103-104

1. Catherine likes sugar and cream in her coffee.
2. The doctors' conference ended with dinner and entertainment.
3. The actors' pictures are on the poster.
4. The performers felt better after the concert.
5. Mr. Arthur answered my letter.
6. I'd rather go to the bakery later.

Key Points 3

日本人はこの [ər] の発音については，日本語の「ア」を [ər] の代わりに用いる傾向があるので，米語の発音の場合は特に注意が必要である。例えば，afternoon が「アフタアヌーン」とか，brother が「プラザア」という発音になりがちなので「ア」とはっきり発音しないようにする。

3 [ə:r] ([ɚ:]) (Mid Central Unrounded Vowel)

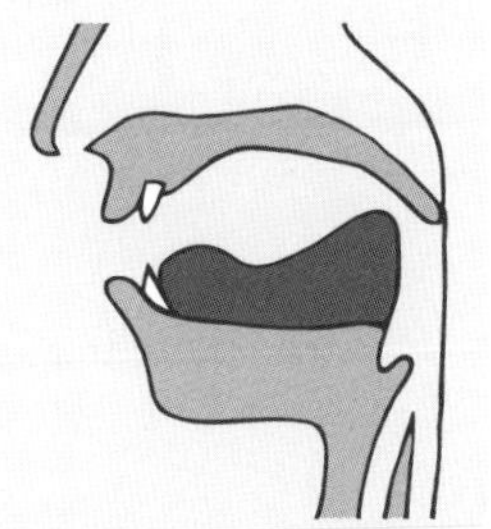

口を少し開き，舌を後方に持ち上げて，[アー] と発音し，[r] の響きの音にする。([ɑ:r] と混同しないように注意する。) イギリス英語ではこの [r] は発音されない。

A. Words (1) 105-106

Initial	Medial	Final
earn	bird	fir
early	girl	fur
irk	merchant	her
urge	serve	prefer
urn	work	refer

B. Words (2) 107-108

journal, amateur, colonel [kə́:rnl], courtesy, myrtle (〔植〕ギンバイカ；祝いの木)

C. Sentences 109-110

1. First come, first served.《諺》(早い者勝ち)
2. The early bird catches the worm.《諺》(早起きは三文の得)
3. We heard Mr. Herbert got hurt in the acccident happened last Thursday.
4. Burt studied German in his third term at the university.
5. Germaine went to church with her father.

Nursery Rhyme 10 111

Little kitty, purring kitty,
With your fur so pretty,
Tell me, kitty, why you're purring,
Purring on my lap.*

*VT 法による英語発音指導教本より

D. Contrast between [ər] and [əːr]. 112

1. Beginners study conversation in their first semester.
2. You certainly were thirsty after the concert!
3. Sherlock is good at solving murder mysteries.
4. Ms. Butterworth drives a purple convertible.
5. Heather is nervous about forgetting her words.
6. On Thursday last week Mr. Fensler turned thirty.

Poem 3 113

EXTREMES

A little boy once played so loud
That the thunder, up in a thundercloud,
Said, "Since I can't be heard, why, then,
I'll never, never thunder again!"

And a little girl once kept so still
That she heard a fly on the window sill
Whisper and say to a ladybird,
"She's the stillest child I've ever heard!"

——James Whitcomb Riley

Exercise 9

Listen to the audio and read the following passages transcribed in phonetic symbols, concentrating on [ə], [ər] and [əːr]. Then write them in ordinary spelling.

1. Sir Isaac Newton

114

wʌn mɔərniŋ səːr aizək n(j)uːtən wəz θiŋkiŋ diːpli ouvər ə difikəlt prɑbləm in hiz ruːm // hiz hauskiːpər fiərd ðət sou lɔːŋ ə fæstiŋ wəd indʒər (h)iz helθ / sou sent ə sərvənt tə bɔil ən eg in hiz stʌdi // səːr aizək / hauevər / wəd nɑt əlau hər tə stei / sou ʃiː left ði eg bai ðə said əv səːr aizəks wɑtʃ ən ðə teibl / æskiŋ him tə let it bɔil θriː minits // səm taim leitər ʃiː went tə siː if hiː həd iːtn ði eg / ənd faund səːr aizək stændiŋ bai ðə faiər / wið ði eg in hiz hænd ən ðə wɑtʃ bɔiliŋ in ðə pæn //

2. Heavier Still

115

“ðis letərz tuː hevi” / sed ðə poust ɑːfis kləːrk // “juːl hæf tə put ənʌðər stæmp ən it” //

“hwɑts ðə gud əv ðæt?” / æskt ðə mæn // “if ai stik ənʌðər stæmp ɑn it / ðætl meik ðə letər heviər stil / wount it?” //

注 // は文末のピリオドの位置を、／はカンマの位置をそれぞれ示している。

Lesson 10

Diphthongs

1 [ai]

日本語の［ア］より舌の位置を低くして口を少し大きく 開き強く［ a ］と発音し，そのあとに軽く［ i ］をそえる。（［愛］のように後の［ i ］をはっきりと発音したり，［ a ］と［ i ］と を切り離したりせず全体として一音のように発音する。）

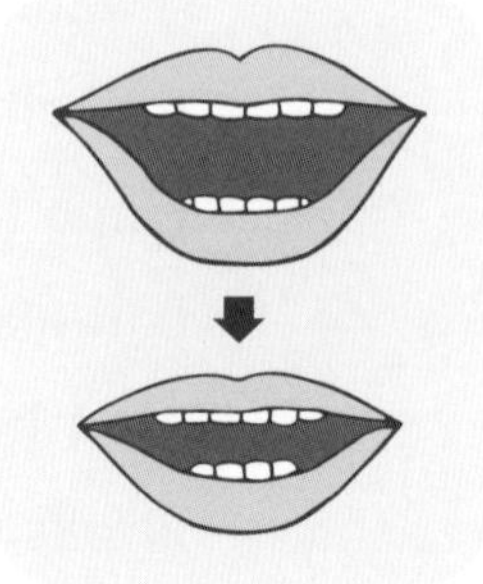

A. Words (1) 116

Initial	Medial	Final
ice	cycle	buy
iron	dial	cry
island	find	high
eyes	guide	my
I	height	tie

B. Words (2) 117

aisle [ail], choir [kwaiər], idea, isle, quiet, reply, sigh

C. Sentences 118

1. A stitch in time saves nine.《諺》（きょうの一針あすの十針）
2. Make hay while the sun shines.《諺》（好機をのがすな）
3. My wife Irene and I dined on Friday night.
4. Look at the kite high up in the sky!
5. She might buy a nice designer tie for that guy.
6. I might go to a nice, tiny, isolated island for a change.
7. Out of sight, out of mind.《諺》（去る者は日々に疎し）

Nursery Rhymes 11 119

(a) Star light, star bright,
First star I see tonight,
I wish I may, I wish I might,
Have the wish I wish tonight.

(b) Queen, Queen Caroline,
Washed her hair in turpentine.
Turpentine made it shine,
Queen, Queen Caroline.

2 [au]

唇をやや広く開いて [a] を強くいったあとに [u] を軽くそえる。この [u] は単母音の [u] ほど唇をまるめないので，聞いた感じは [ao] に似ている。

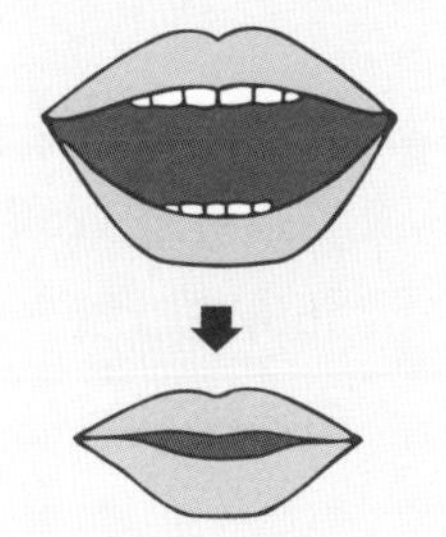

A. Words (1) 120

Initial	Medial	Final
our	around	allow
ouch	crown	bow
ounce	drown	wow
out	pound	plow, plough
owl	power	thou

B. Words (2) 121

bough, drought, foul, fowl

C. Sentences 122

1. The outlaw wasn't allowed to come back to the town.
2. Do you know how many ounces make a pound?
3. Let's sing "The Sound of Silence" again, louder!
4. You are finding out how to pronounce English vowels.
5. Behold the fowls of the air. (Matthew 6 : 26)

Nursery Rhymes 12 123

See-saw, sacradown,
Which is the way to London town?
One foot up and the other foot down
That is the way to London town.

3 [ɔi]

日本語の［オ］よりも少し口を大きく開き唇をまるめて突き出して強く[ɔ]と発音し，そのあと軽く[i]をそえて[ɔi]と発音する。（boy を［ボーイ］と長くしすぎても，また[ɔ]をあまり短くしてもいけない。）

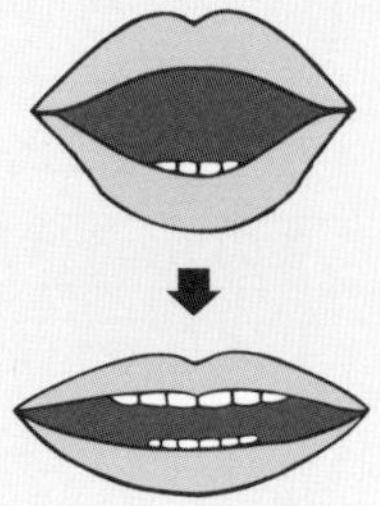

A. Words (1) 124

Initial	Medial	Final
oil	avoid	annoy
oiler	choice	boy
oink	poison	joy
ointment	royal	destroy
oyster	voyage	toy

B. Words (2) 125

buoy [bɔi]（ブイ）, buoyant（浮きやすい，快活な）, employ

C. Sentences 126

1. I enjoyed the oysters fried in soy bean oil.
2. Boys, pick up your toys!
3. My choice is this oily part of the tuna fish, called *toro* in Japanese.
4. The spoiled boy made a noise that annoyed his sister, Joy.
5. There is no royal road to learning. 《諺》（学問に王道なし）

Nursery Rhymes 13 127

All work and no play makes Jack a dull boy;
All play and no work makes Jack a mere toy.

4 [iər] ([iɚ])

日本語の［エ］と［イ］の中間音のような [i] で始めて，そのあとに [ə] をそえ，さらに軽く [r] の音を響かせる。[ər] は軽く発音することと，[iər] を二音節に切って発音しないことが大切。

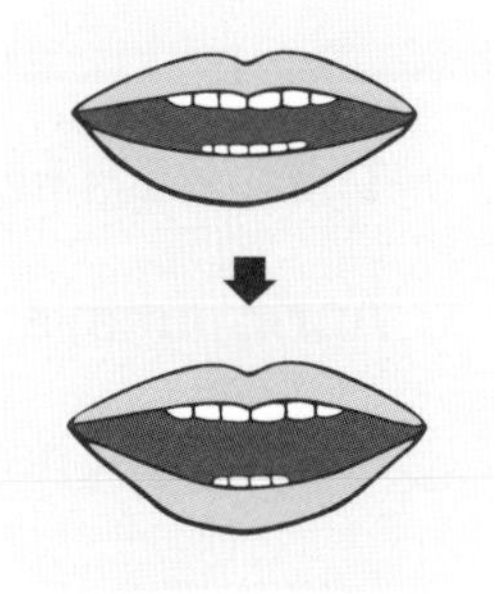

A. Words (1) 128-129

Initial	Medial	Final
ear	beard	cheer
earring	cheerful	clear
earmuffs	merely	hear
eeriee, eery	tearful	tear (*n.*)
era	weird	year

B. Words (2) 130-131

cashier, fierce, gear, premier, queer, souvenir, volunteer

C. Sentences 132-133

1. This year Mr. Greer has come here often for the clear weather.
2. The engineers drink beer near the souvenir shop.
3. You should try to create an atmosphere of cheerfulness.
4. After visiting the museum, the premier went to the pier.
5. Experience keeps a dear school.《諺》（人はひどい目にあって利口になる）

Thirty days hath September,
April, June, and November;
All the rest have thirty-one,
Excepting February alone,
And that has twenty-eight days clear
And twenty-nine in each leap year.

TURKEY TIME

Thanksgiving Day will soon be here;
It comes around but once a year,
If I could only have my way,
We'd have thanksgiving every day!

THE OLD MAN WITH A BEARD

There was an old man with a beard
Who said, "It is just as I feared!
Two owls and a hen,
Four larks and a wren,
Have all built their nests in my beard!"

Edward Lear

5 [ɛər] ([ɛɚ])

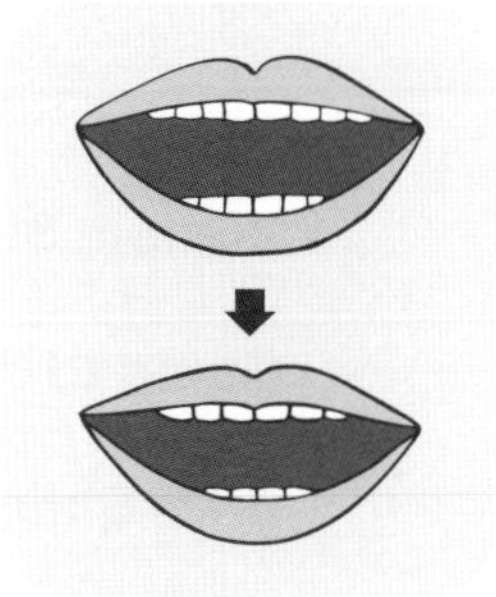

[e] よりも口を大きく開いた [ɛ] で始めてそのあとに [ər] を軽くそえる。二音節に切らないこと。

A. Words (1) 135-136

Initial	Medial	Final
air	parent	care
area	rarity	chair
ere	scarce	fair
heir	scared	stair
Eire	various	there

B. Words (2) 137-138

beware, dairy, dare, vary, questionnaire

C. Sentences 139-140

1. Mary wasn't aware of the embarrassing affair.
2. The spareribs are over there by the marinated herring.
3. The parents of the fair-haired heir were billionaires.
4. Be careful not to tear the rare books!
5. Clare went to the fair with Marian.

Nursery Rhymes 15 141

(a) Simple Simon met a pieman,
Going to the fair;
Says Simple Simon to the pieman,
Let me taste your ware.

(b) The first day of Christmas,
My true love sent to me
A partridge in a pear tree.

(c) Dickery, dickery, dare
The pig flew up in the air;
The man in brown
Soon brought him down,
Dickery, dickery, dare.

(d) Here is the church, and here is the steeple;
Open the door and here are the people,
Here is the parson going upstairs,
And here he is a-saying his prayers.

6 [ɔər] ([ɔɚ]), [ɔːr]

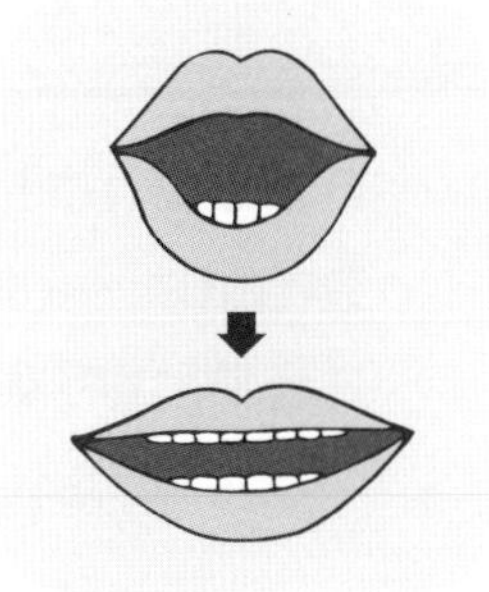

日本語の［オ］よりも口を少し大きく開いて発音される[ɔ]で始めてそのあとに軽く[ər]をそえる。二音節に切り離さないこと。イギリス英語では[ɔː]と発音されることが多い。

A. Words (1) 142-143

Initial	Medial	Final
or	born	door
oar	corner	four
ore	corn	more
orbit	course	soar
oral	morning	war

B. Words (2) 144-145

adore, floor, orchestra, roar, tore, sword, therefore, toward

C. Sentences 146-147

1. The soaring planes roared toward the airport.
2. Fourteen sophomores went to Baltimore.
3. George snored on the floor till morning.
4. Outdoor goods are sold at that store.
5. Please order four more pork chops.

Nursery Rhymes 16 148

Georgie Porgie, pudding and pie,
Kissed the girls and made them cry;
When the boys came out to play,
Georgie Porgie ran away.

7 [uər] ([uɚ]), [juər]

日本語の［ウ］よりもっと唇をまるめて，口笛を吹くように前に突き出した [u] で始め，そのあとに [ər] を軽くそえる。これも二音節に切り離さないこと。イギリス英語では [uər] の代りに [ɔː] も用いられる傾向がある。

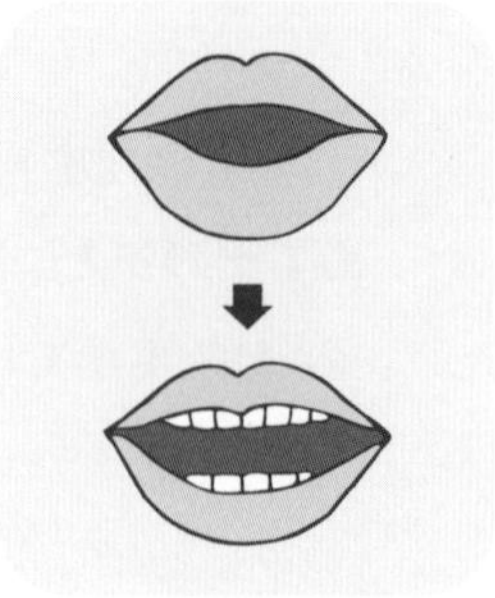

A. Words (1) 149-150

Initial	Medial	Final
NONE	curious	cure
—	during	endure
—	poorer	mature
—	surely	obscure
—	tourist	you're

B. Words (2) 151-152

insure, premature

-ur, -ure, -eur, 等の綴り字および your は [juər] と発音される。（p.122 参照）

C. Sentences 153-154

1. The pure air of the moor is a sure cure.
2. I hope you'll feel safe and secure on the next tour to Europe.
3. During the summer, many tourists flock to the famous curio shop.
4. The new young man at the insurance company is very mature.
5. If you're sure you can endure it, let's take a long tour.
6. Blessed are the poor in spirit: for theirs is the kingdom of heaven. (Matthew 5 : 3)
7. Blessed are the pure in heart: for they shall see God. (Matthew 5 : 8)

D. Passage for reading (3)

Listen to the audio and read the following. 155-156

Mr. Knott was a teacher. He taught in a big school in London. He lived away from the school, so he was usually quite tired when he got home. At nine o'clock one evening, when he was in bed, the telephone rang in the hall of his small house, so he went downstairs, picked up the telephone and said, 'This is Whitebridge 3165. Who's speaking, please?'

'Watt,' a man answered.

'What's your name, please?' said Mr. Knott.

'Watt's my name,' was the answer.

'Yes, I asked you that. What's your name?' Mr. Knott said again.

'I told you. Watt's my name,' said the other man. 'Are you Jack Smith?'

'No, I'm Knott,' answered Mr. Knott.

'Will you give me your name, please?' said Mr. Watt.

'Will Knott,' answered Mr. Knott.

Both Mr. Watt and Mr. Will Knott put their telephones down angrily and thought, 'That was a rude, stupid man!'

(Adopted from *Elementary Stories for Reproduction 2* by L. A. Hill)

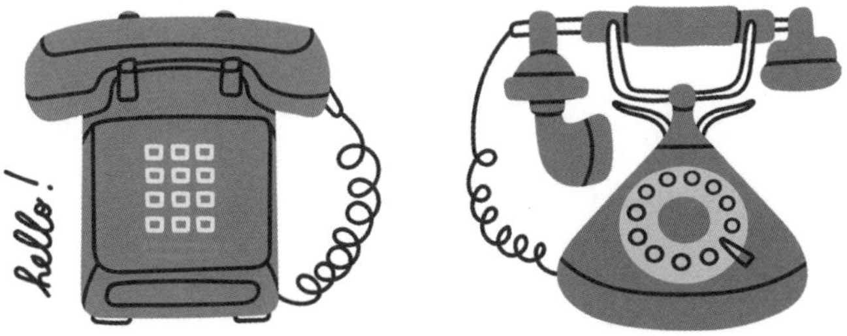

Exercise 10

Write two words in the blanks that have the same sound but different meanings. Listen to the example.

Homophones（同音異形異義語）　e.g. [pɛər] pair, pear　157

1. [bɛər] ________ ________
2. [bəːrθ] ________ ________
3. [bluː] ________ ________
4. [breik] ________ ________
5. [fɛər] ________ ________
6. [hiːl] ________ ________
7. [hiər] ________ ________
8. [auər] ________ ________
9. [nou] ________ ________
10. [led] ________ ________
11. [meil] ________ ________
12. [nait] ________ ________
13. [nʌn] ________ ________
14. [peil] ________ ________
15. [red] ________ ________
16. [riːd] ________ ________
17. [siːn] ________ ________
18. [sʌm] ________ ________
19. [sʌn] ________ ________
20. [ðɛər] ________ ________

CHAPTER I

VOWELS & CONSONANTS

II. CONSONANTS & SEMIVOWELS

FAIRY TALES
COSMOS
encyclopedia
POEMS
dino
ABC
BIRDS
princess
ATLAS
ADVENTURE

英語の子音・半母音分類表

Manner of Articulation		Point of Articulation						
		bilabial	**labio-dental**	**inter-dental**	**alveolar**	**alveo-palatal**	**velar**	**glottal**
stop 閉鎖音	(vl)	p			t		k	
	(vd)	b			d		g	
fricative 摩擦音	(vl)		f	θ	s	ʃ		h
	(vd)		v	ð	z (r)	ʒ		
affricate 破擦音	(vl)					tʃ		
	(vd)					dʒ		
lateral 側音	(vd)				l			
nasal 鼻音	(vd)	m			n		ŋ	
semivowel 半母音	(vd)	w			r	j		

vl = voiceless（無声音），vd = voiced（有声音）

子音・半母音発音記号一覧表

158

1. [p] pen
2. [b] book
3. [t] ten
4. [d] day
5. [k] come
6. [g] good
7. [f] face
8. [v] very
9. [θ] thanks
10. [ð] this
11. [s] sun
12. [z] zoo
13. [ʃ] ship
14. [ʒ] usual
15. [h] hear
16. [tʃ] child
17. [dʒ] just
18. [l] love ([ɫ] oil)
19. [m] man
20. [n] name
21. [ŋ] sing
22. [w] way
23. [r] rich
24. [j] young

Lesson 11 [p]–[b]

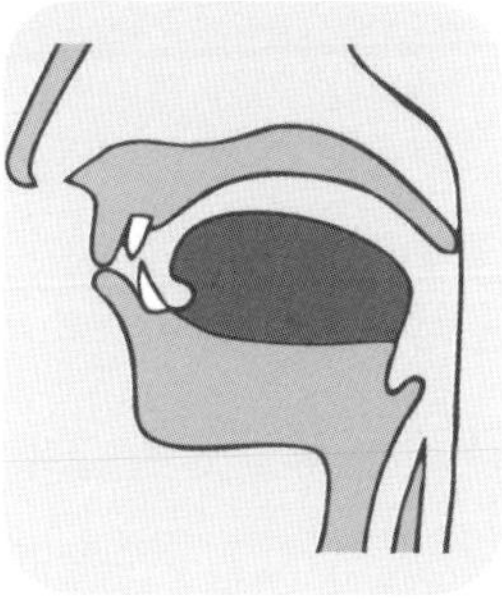

両唇を強く閉じて口の中に息をため，唇の間から急激に息を出して発音する。語頭では息をパッと出し強く破裂させる。

1 [p] (Voiceless Bilabial Stop)

A. Words (1) 159

Initial	Medial	Final
pick	appoint	tip
patient	apology	map
punctual	capable	hope
purchase	deposit	top
popular	suppose	soup

B. Words (2) 160

pump, apple, happy, shopping, upper, grape, shepherd

＊黙字 p を含む語

cupboard, pneumonia, psalm, psychology, raspberry, receipt

C. Consonant-clusters 161

Initial	plastic, pleasure, plug, practice, prize, proof
Medial	April, surprise, captain, caption, chapter, option
Final	gulp, help, yelp, crisp, grasp, jump

D. Sentences 162

1. Would you pass me the potatoes, please?
2. Paul apologized for his poor performance.
3. Ping-pong is a popular sport in Japan.
4. Pop in and see me if you happen to be passing by!
5. I can't keep up with these piles of paper work.

2 [b] (Voiced Bilabial Stop)

A. Words (1) 163

Initial	Medial	Final
big	cabbage	cab
busy	labor	club
bad	member	robe
bought	rabbit	disturb
boots	subway	tube

B. Words (2) 164

Bob, bathtub, hobby, ribbon, globe

*黙字 b を含む語

bomb, climb, comb, debt, doubt, lamb, tomb, thumb

C. Consonant-clusters 165

Initial	block, blood, blue, brain, breakfast, bright
Medial	absent, absurd, abstract, probably, problem, public
Final	bulb

D. Sentences 166

1. I want to buy butter and bacon for breakfast.
2. Do you have enough beer for Bob and Betty?
3. Nice to meet you, Barbara. This is my husband, Bob.
4. How about another bottle of beer, Ben?
5. This is your bedroom. And here's the bathroom.

3 Contrast between [p] and [b]

A. Words 167

1. pair—bear	4. pound—bound	7. rope—robe	10. rip—rib
2. peach—beach	5. prick—brick	8. cap—cab	
3. planned—bland	6. simple—symbol	9. tap—tab	

B. Sentences 168

1. The Peabodys' pig is very big.
2. Why don't you buy this apple pie?
3. The driver's cap matches his cab.
4. There are some peach trees along the beach.
5. This phonetic symbol is simple.

4 Sound Transitions

A. Phrases 169

1. **[p] + [p]** : cheap pencils, deep pond, keep praying, sharp point, sleep peacefully, stop playing
2. **[p] + [t/d]** : hope to, stop today, drop down, top drawer
3. **[b] + [b]** : job benefits, lab building, rob banks
4. **[p] + Vowel** : a cup of tea, cup and saucer, keep in, pop in, stop in, stop it, up and down

B. Sentences 170

1. Stop pushing me, please.
2. Phillip Peterson won the singing competition last week.
3. Would you like a cup of tea, Beth?
4. Do you like Barb best?
5. Bob baked bread and biscuits by himself.

Tongue Twister 1 171

Peter Piper picked a peck of pickled peppers;

Did Peter Piper pick a peck of pickled peppers?

If Peter Piper picked a peck of pickled peppers,

Where's the peck of pickled peppers Peter Piper picked?

Exercise 11

A. Listen carefully and circle the letter of the words or sentences which are correctly pronounced.

172

1. a) pay b) bay c) pay
2. a) buy b) buy c) pie
3. a) beer b) peer c) peer
4. a) cap b) cap c) cap
5. a) tab b) tap c) tab
6. a) Don't you have a long robe?
   b) Don't you have a long rope?
   c) Don't you have a long rope?
7. a) Would you give me a pack?
   b) Would you give me a pack?
   c) Would you give me a pack?

B. Listen carefully and fill in the blanks.

173

1. Bill is going on the (   ).
2. My uncle has a big (   ).
3. The boat went up (   ) down over the waves.
4. You have to keep (   ) studying until you pass.
5. I asked them to (   ) talking, but they just went on.
6. We shouldn't (   ) Bob waiting so long.
7. I had a (   ) (   ) for a few weeks.
8. He is one of the (   ) (   ) singers in Japan.

Lesson 12 [t]–[d]

1 [t] (Voiceless Alveolar Stop)

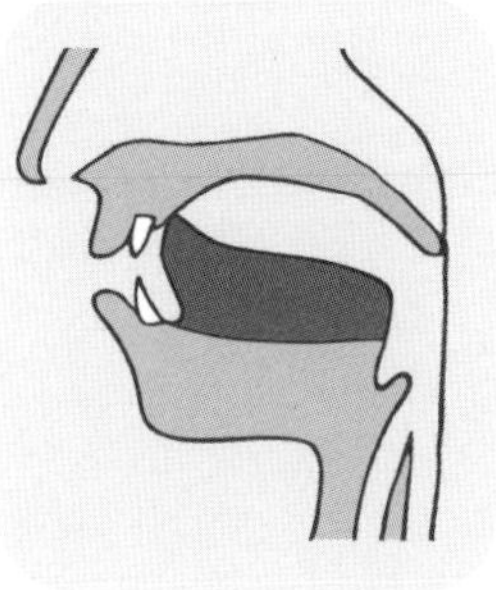

舌先を上歯茎に押しつけて息をため，急に舌を離し息を出して発音する。語頭では息をパッと出し強く破裂させる。
[ti] [tu] と [di] [du] は日本語にないので特に注意すること。

A. Words (1) 174

Initial	Medial	Final
ticket	attend	wheat
tennis	attitude	sit
touch	continue	planet
turn	matter	taught
tooth	potato	foot

B. Words (2) 175

steel, tip, tour, tourist, tube, tulip, batter, cotton, setting, Thailand, Thames, Thomas, debt, doubt, yacht

＊黙字 t を含む語

castle, chestnut, Christmas, fasten, hasten, listen, mustn't, nestle, often, whistle, wrestler

C. Consonant-clusters 176

Initial	train, travel, trouble, twenty, twin, twist
Medial	football, gentleman, neutral, notebook, outline
Final	contact, Egypt, gift, guest, result, text, vacant

D. Sentences 177

1. Will you tell Grandma it's time for tea?
2. Try not to lose your credit card.
3. The doctor told me to take two tablets every eight hours.
4. Today's teenagers tend to waste too much time watching YouTube videos.
5. Don't put off till tomorrow what you can do today.

2 [d] (Voiced Alveolar Stop)

A. Words (1) 178

Initial	Medial	Final
dinner	editor	fade
dirty	India	said
dawn	indeed	card
dull	medicine	wood
duty	random	mode

B. Words (2) 179

dilemma, Hindu, address, ladder, sudden, could, should, would

＊黙字 d を含む語

handkerchief, handsome, Wednesday, Windsor

☆脱落を起こしやすい d を含む語

good-by, grandma, handbag, kindness, landlady, landscape, Lindberg, sandwich

C. Consonant-clusters 180

Initial	drama, dress, drink, drive, drop, dwell, dwindle
Medial	handball, endless, mindless, children, hundred
Final	cold, field, world, demand, intend, second

D. Sentences 181

1. Every dog has his day. 《諺》（だれにでも得意な時はあるもの）
2. Did you say good-bye to your host family?
3. My husband and I like all kinds of bread.
4. A friend in need is a friend indeed. 《諺》（まさかの時の友こそ真の友）
5. “Do you feel like having a drink?” “Good idea! I’d love one.”

3 Contrast between [t] and [d]

A. Words 182

1. try—dry
2. tear—dear
3. tense—dense
4. latter—ladder
5. metal—medal
6. writing—riding
7. putting—pudding
8. bright—bride
9. sight—side
10. cart—card

B. Sentences 183

1. I'll try to make the shirt dry in the sun.
2. This medal is made of heavy metal.
3. I went shopping downtown yesterday afternoon.
4. The bride was wearing a big bright diamond.
5. The company has planned to plant a factory in Los Angeles.

4 Sound Transitions

A. Phrases 184

1. **[t] + [t/d]** : at two hot tea, part-time, hot dog, white dress
2. **[t] + [b]** : East Bank, get back, heart break, hot bath
3. **[d]+ [d/t]** : cold day, good driver, good time, round table
4. **[d] + [b]** : good boy, good-bye, had better, red bag
5. **[t/d] + [j]** : don't you, not yet, and you, did you, would you
6. **[d/t] + Vowel** : in front of, not at all, find out, kind of

B. Sentences 185

1. Did you have a good time, Ted?
2. I'll meet you in front of the Trust Bank at two p.m.
3. Would you like some more hot tea, Trudy?
4. Won't you sit down and eat a hot dog, Todd?
5. You'd better leave here at ten if you want to get to work on time.

Key Points 4 186-187

米音の [t] [d] の発音

　米音では強勢のある母音と強勢のない母音の間にある [t] は有声化したり，弾音化したりして、[d] や日本語のラ行音に近い音になる。

　　（例）atom, better, latter, matter, thirty, water

また，[n] と母音または [l] の間にある [t] [d] は脱落する傾向がある。

　　（例）gentle, twenty, wanted, candidate, windmill

Exercise 12

A. Listen carefully and circle the letter of the words or sentences which are correctly pronounced.

1. a) tried b) tried c) dried 188
2. a) putting b) putting c) pudding
3. a) latter b) ladder c) latter
4. a) seat b) seed c) seed
5. a) dead b) debt c) dead
6. a) Can I borrow your card?
   b) Can I borrow your cart?
   c) Can I borrow your card?
7. a) Would you show me the *Times*?
   b) Would you show me the dimes?
   c) Would you show me the *Times*?

B. Listen carefully and fill in the blanks. 189

1. I've just (   ) (   ) bad (   ).
2. We had a (   ) (   ) getting (   ) the airport on account (   ) the traffic accident.
3. Twinkle, twinkle, (   ) (   )!
   How I (   ) (   ) (   ) are!
   Up above the (   ) so high,
   Like a (   ) in the sky.
   Twinkle, twinkle (   ) (   )!
   How I (   ) (   ) (   ) are!

Lesson 13 [k]–[g]

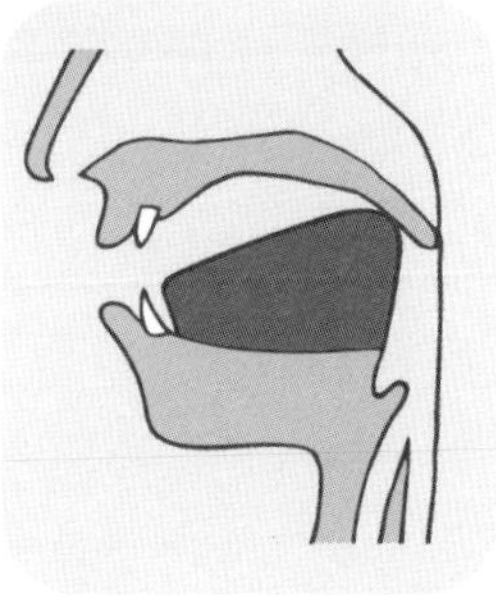

舌の奥を軟口蓋に押し当てて息をとめ，急に奥舌を下げ，息を［クッ］と出して発音する。語頭では息をパッと出し強く破裂させる。

1 [k] (Voiceless Velar Stop)

A. Words (1) 190

Initial	Medial	Final
key	account	clock
kitchen	liquor	luck
kettle	occasion	public
country	package	technique
cause	pocket	unique

B. Words (2) 191

scale, scarcely, accustom, scholar, stomach-ache, attack, nickel, sick, acquaintance, conquer, mosquito, except, walk

＊黙字 c, k を含む語

Connecticut, muscle, kneel, knit, knock, know

C. Consonant-clusters 192

Initial	claim, clock, credit, crowd, quarter, question, quiz
Medial	accident, acquire, inquire, require, recruit, sacrifice, direction, lecture, reaction, exercise, expect, luxury

D. Sentences 193

1. All work and no play makes Jack a dull boy. 《諺》（よく学びよく遊べ）
2. I'd like Mike to clean the kitchen.
3. I couldn't find any Christmas cards in the bookcase.
4. Take your coat off, if you like. It's warm here in October.
5. Dick took care not to catch cold before the concert.

2 [g] (Voiced Velar Stop)

A. Words (1) 194

Initial	Medial	Final
guitar	baggage	fatigue
gear	forgive	flag
guess	Michigan	plug
gasoline	negative	smog
guide	organ	zigzag

B. Words (2) 195

signature, giggle, argue, colleague, Ghana, ghost, exact, exhaust

＊黙字 g, gh を含む語

design, foreign, reign, sign, daughter, neighbor, sigh, though, through, weight

C. Consonant-clusters 196

Initial	glad, glove, glue, grand, grape, grass, group
Medial	Anglican, Anglo-Saxon, English, angry, congress, hungry

D. Sentences 197

1. We grow grapes in our garden.
2. The guard at the embassy gate gave me a friendly look.
3. The language course will begin in August.
4. The foreigner in my neighborhood teaches Greek at the college.
5. I feel hungry now. Could you get me some eggs and grapes?

3 Contrast between [k] and [g]

A. Words 198

1. could—good
2. cap—gap
3. class—glass
4. card—guard
5. coal—goal
6. lock—log
7. leak—league
8. lack—lag
9. pick—pig
10. frock—frog

B. Sentences 199

1. Thousands of people came to the stadium for the game.
2. Gary is carrying a rice bag on his back.
3. Kate is waiting at the garden gate.
4. I wish I could be a good cook.
5. I saw two dogs running toward the docks.

4 Sound Transitions

A. Phrases 200

1. **[k] + [k]** : black cat, black coffee, bookcase, look carefully, make cookies, pink coat, rock candy
2. **[k] + Vowel** : back up, knock out, look after, look at, look up a word, pick it up, take it easy
3. **[g] + [g]** : big game, big garden, big gorilla, big grapes
4. **[g] + Vowel** : a tug of war, big apple, dig a hole, dog-eared, drag a field, egg apple, egg and spoon race

B. Sentences 201

1. I asked my sister to look after the baby for a while.
2. "I hear you got a new black coat."
   "Oh, it's nothing to speak of."
3. The temple is famous for its wonderful big garden.
4. We enjoyed an egg and spoon race.
5. How much are these big apples in the basket?
6. Carol has a cup of black coffee at ten every morning.
7. You look tired. Take care of yourself.

Key Points 5　202

有気音（帯気音）（Aspiration）の有無

(1) [p][t][k] が強勢のある音節の頭にある時は，息を強くはきだす。

（例）come, key, kind, pen, pin, put, ten, took, top

(2) 強勢のない音節の初頭や音節の末尾では，気息は弱まるか無くなる。

（例）check, music, picnic, perform, pocket, shop, sit, sleep

(3) [p] [t] [k] が [s] の次にある時は気息音はなくなる。

（例）Spain, speak, stay, steel, skill, sky

Key Points 6　203

無声音 (Voiceless) と有声音 (Voiced) の違い

発音する時に声門を通る空気が声帯を振動させれば有声音となり，声帯を振動させなければ無声音となる (p.10 の図)。母音は全て有声音であるが，子音は有声音と無声音があり（p.63)，例えば，[p]-[b], [t]-[d], [k]-[g], [f]-[v], [tʃ]-[dʒ] はそれぞれ無声音と有声音の関係である。これによって次のような最小対立（minimal pair）をなしている。

（例）peach-beach, town-down, cap-gap, fast-vast, cheap-jeep

Nursery Rhymes 17, 18 204

(17) THIS LITTLE PIG WENT TO MARKET

This little pig went to market,
This little pig stayed home,
This little pig had roast beef,
This little pig had none;
This little pig cried “Wee! wee! wee!”
All the way home.

(18) THREE LITTLE KITTENS

Three little kittens, they lost their mittens,
So they began to cry,
“O mother dear, come here, come here,
For we have lost our mittens.”
“Lost your mittens? You naughty kittens!
Then you shall have not pie.”
“Miaou! Miaou! We shall have no pie.”

Three little kittens, they found their mittens,
So they began to cry,
“O mother dear, come here, come here,
For we have found our mittens.”
“Found your mittens? You good little kittens,
Now you shall have some pie.”
“Prrrr! Prrrr! Now we shall have some pie.”

Exercise 13

A. Listen carefully and circle the letter of the words or sentences which are correctly pronounced.

1. a) gold b) gold c) cold 205
2. a) coast b) ghost c) coast
3. a) angle b) ankle c) angle
4. a) back b) bag c) bag
5. a) Is this your coat?
   b) Is this your goat?
   c) Is this your coat?
6. a) Don't put it in the bag.
   b) Don't put it it in the bag.
   c) Don't put it in the back.
7. a) The policeman has lost his clubs.
   b) The policeman has lost his gloves.
   c) The policeman has lost his clubs.

B. Listen carefully and fill in the blanks. 206

1. Our teacher had come by the time I (   ) (   ) (   ).
2. He brought his (   ) (   ) outside.
3. Do you (   ) it will be (   )?
4. (   ) (   ) will be ready for sale in a few days.
5. I don't (   ) (   ) coffee.

Lesson 14

[f]–[v]

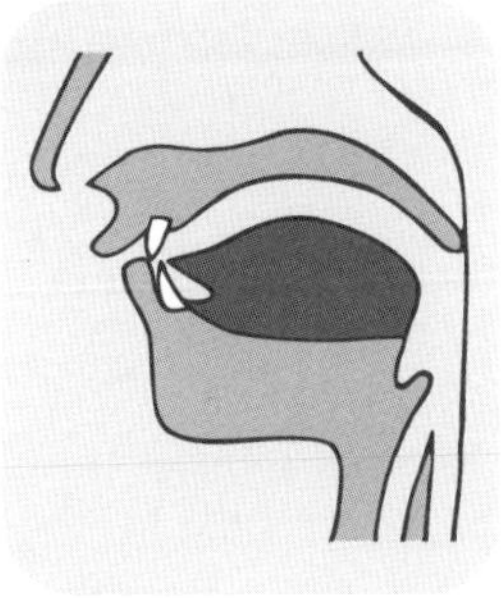

上歯で下唇を軽くおさえ，そのすき間から［フッ］と息を強く出して発音する。
日本語の［フ］［ブ］にならないように注意すること。

1 [f] (Voiceless Labio-dental Fricative)

A. Words (1) 207

Initial	Medial	Final
feet	afford	sheriff
fence	effect	chief
farm	office	staff
forty	refuse	leaf
food	suffer	proof

B. Words (2) 208

elephant, emphasis, graph, hyphen, orphan, pamphlet, pharmacy, philosophy, photograph, telephone, sapphire, cough, enough, laugh, rough, tough

C. Consonant-clusters 209

Initial	flash, flight, floor, free, fresh, front, fruit
Medial	after, fifteen, fifty, laughter, reflect, soften
Final	golf, gulf, self, shelf, wolf

D. Sentences 210

1. Is this your first flight to San Francisco?
2. I don't feel like having breakfast this morning.
3. You can find the frozen food shelf near the fish counter.
4. My father has been suffering from a fever for four days.
5. A fire broke out on the fifth floor of a famous hotel in Florida.

2 [v] (Voiced Labio-dental Fricative)

A. Words (1) 211

Initial	Medial	Final
village	average	above
very	invite	improve
value	private	move
volunteer	service	receive
vote	severe	save

B. Words (2) 212

of, oven, Stephen, Stephenson, vacant, Venus, Vienna, Vietnam, view, vitamin, vogue, voltage, volume, voyage

C. Consonant-clusters 213

Final involve, resolve, revolve, shelve, solve, valve

D. Sentences 214

1. The voice of the people is the voice of God.
2. Vivian loved to travel through the deep valley in the Grand Canyon.
3. I was tired of reading, so I watched a movie on TV.
4. I'm not rich enough to afford such an expensive violin.
5. The view from the villa in the village is fantastic.

3 -1. Contrast between [f] and [v]

A. Words 215

1. fail—veil
2. fast—vast
3. ferry—very
4. few—view
5. rifle—rival
6. refuse—reviews
7. safe—save
8. leaf—leave
9. half—have
10. proof—prove

B. Sentences 216

1. The ferryboat was very crowded.
2. Not a few people hold views against the matter.
3. I have half a mind to invite Fran for New Year's Eve.

3-2. Contrast between [h] and [f]

A. Words 217

1. hair—fair
2. hall—fall
3. hate—fate
4. heat—feet
5. hill—fill
6. hit—fit
7. hold—fold
8. horse—force
9. honey—funny
10. her—fur

B. Sentences 218

1. Fortunately, his hound was found safe in the house.
2. The frost did much harm on the fruit farm.
3. The city hall will be rebuilt in the fall next year.

3-3. Contrast between [b] and [v]

A. Words 219

1. bend—vend
2. berry—very
3. best—vest
4. boat—vote
5. bow—vow
6. marble—marvel
7. ban—van
8. TB—TV
9. bolt—volt
10. curb—curve

B. Sentences 220

1. Did you say TV or TB?
2. I vote we take a boat.
3. This berry is very sweet.

4 Sound Transitions

A. Phrases 221

1. **[f] + [f]** : enough food, graph 4, rough flight, tough farmer
2. **[f] + [v]** : brief view, half volum, life vest
3. **[v] + [v]** : conservative voters, five voters, leave very early
4. **[v] + [f]** : brave fighters, five fingers, give food
5. **[v] + Vowel** : give it to me, live in a village, love affair

B. Sentences 222

1. You'll receive an invitation card to the party in a couple of days.
2. This village has a lot of conservative voters.
3. I've found a very useful dictionary.
4. The love of money is the root of all evil. 《諺》（金銭欲は諸悪の根源）
5. They were lost in the woods but they had enough food for a few days.

C. Listen and Memorize 223

The Arrow and the Song by H. W. Longfellow

I shot an arrow into the air,
It fell to earth, I knew not where;
For, so swiftly it flew, the sight
Could not follow it in its flight.

I breathed a song into the air.
It fell to earth, I knew not where;
For who has sight so keen and strong,
That it can follow the flight of song?

Long, long afterward, in an oak
I found the arrow, still unbroke;
And the song, from beginning to end,
I found again in the heart of a friend.

Key Points 7 224

特に唇を使う子音

英語の次の子音および半母音は日本語の子音よりも特に唇をよく動かせて発音する。

(1) 唇を丸めて前へつきだす。

[w]: wolf, woman, wood, wool, worry

[r]: right, road, roof, round, wrong

(2) 唇を丸めてすき間を作る。

[ʃ] [ʒ]: sheep, sheet, ship, casual, usual

(3) 上歯で下唇を軽く押さえてすき間を作る。

[f] [v]: fair, feel, food, very, vote

(4) 唇を強く閉じる。

[m]: main, meet, money, moon, more

Nursery Rhymes 19 225

Monday's child is fair of face,

Tuesday's child is full of grace,

Wednesday's child is full of woe,

Thursday's child has far to go,

Friday's child is loving and giving,

Saturday's child works hard for a living,

And the child that is born on the Sabbath day

Is bonny and blithe, and good and gay.

Exercise 14

A. Listen carefully and circle the letter of the words or sentences which are correctly pronounced.

226

1. a) horse　　b) horse　　c) force
2. a) fill　　b) hill　　c) fill
3. a) leaf　　b) leaf　　c) leave
4. a) view　　b) few　　c) few
5. a) very　　b) berry　　c) very
6. a) best　　b) best　　c) vest
7. a) It's said that the politician bought a boat.
   b) It's said that the politician bought a vote.
   c) It's said that the politician bought a vote.
8. a) He took his rival to the match.
   b) He took his rival to the match.
   c) He took his rifle to the match.

B. Listen carefully and fill in the blanks. 227

S: What (　　　　) of America are you (　　　　)?

J: I'm originally (　　　　) Seattle, Washington. But I now (　　　　) in Dallas, Texas.

S: Dallas, Texas! Did you watch "(　　　　)" on (　　　　) in the (　　　　)?

J: Uh huh.

S: They (　　　　) it in Japan a (　　　　) (　　　　) ago, too.

J: I've (　　　　) (　　　　) that. (　　　　) (　　　　) like the show?

S: Yes, (　　　　) much. But it wasn't very (　　　　) and they (　　　　) (　　　　) (　　　　) the air after (　　　　) a (　　　　) months.

J: I wonder why.

S: I guess it just didn't match Japanese (　　　　) very much.

Lesson 15 [θ]–[ð]

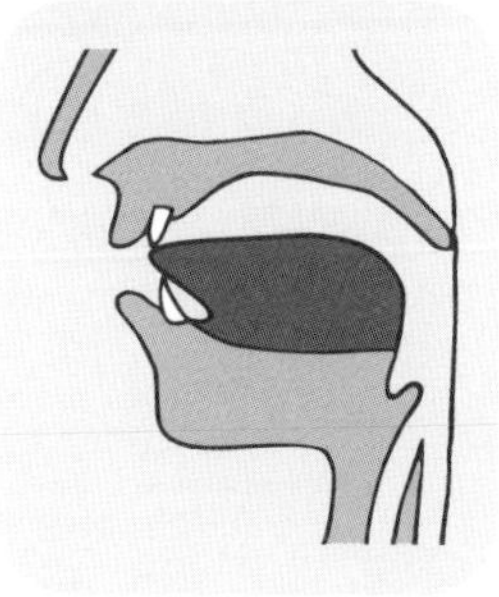

舌先を上の歯先に押しあてたままで，上歯と舌先のすき間から［ス］と息を強く出して発音する。日本語の［ス］［ズ］にならないように注意すること。

1 [θ] (Voiceless Interdental Fricative)

A. Words (1) 228

Initial	Medial	Final
thick	Arthur	birth
theory	author	earth
thousand	Catholic	Elizabeth
thirsty	faithful	mouth
thumb	method	path

B. Words (2) 229

anthem, Athens, Gothic, Marathon, Matthew, nothing, thanks, eighth, fifth, fortieth, hundredth, ninth, third, twelfth

C. Consonant-clusters 230

Initial	thrash, three, thrill, throat, through, throw
Medial	athletics, breathless, monthly, wealthy, worthless
Final	depth, health, length, month, strength, wealth

D. Sentences 231

1. Health is better than wealth. 《諺》（健康は富に勝る）
2. Thank you for the birthday present.
3. Mr. Smith will be thirty-three next Thursday.
4. Nathaniel Hawthorne is the author of *The Scarlet Letter*.
5. Three thousand houses were destroyed by the earthquake in that city last month.

2 [ð] (Voiced Interdental Fricative)

A. Words (1) 232

Initial	Medial	Final
this	bother	breathe
there	further	mouth (*v.*)
that	other	bathe
though	rhythm	clothe
thus	weather	smooth

B. Words (2) 233

(1) Noun [θ]—Verb [ð]

bath—bathe

breath—breathe

cloth—clothe

sooth—soothe

(2) Noun [θ]—Adjective [ð]

north—northern

south—southern

worth—worthy

C. Sentences 234

1. I hope the weather will clear up tomorrow.
2. Both of the brothers take after their mother.
3. I think both their father and mother are healthy.
4. This is the most expensive leather coat in this store.

3 -1. Contrast between [θ] and [ð]

A. Words 235

1. thigh—thy
2. ether—either
3. teeth—teethe
4. wreath—wreathe
5. mouth (*n.*)—mouth (*v.*)

B. Sentences 236

1. We need either alcohol or ether for the chemical exeriment.
2. This teething baby has three new teeth.
3. Could you tell me how to spell the words *thigh* and *thy*?

3 -2. Contrast between [θ] and [t]

A. Words 237

1. three—tree
2. threw—true
3. thrill—trill
4. theme—team
5. both—boat
6. tenth—tent

B. Sentences 238

1. There are three cherry trees in the garden.
2. "Where is Mr. Smith?" "He is on the tenth floor."
3. The need for world peace was the theme of our team.

3 -3. Contrast between [ð] and [d]

A. Words 239

1. they—day
2. there—dare
3. those—doze
4. worthy—wordy
5. breathe—breed
6. thy—die

B. Sentences 240

1. They left Japan the day before yesterday.
2. Those are the students who often doze in class.
3. Dragons can be scary when they breathe fire.

3 -4. Contrast between [z] and [ð]

A. Words 241

1. Zen—then
2. bays—bathe
3. breeze—breathe
4. close—clothe
5. rise—writhe
6. tease—teethe

B. Sentences 242

1. It was Zen that they studied then.
2. You can breathe in a fresh breeze on the hill.
3. These bays are good to bathe in.

4 Sound Transitions

A. Phrases 243

1. **[θ] + [θ]** : the fifth theater, the fourth thief, the fourth Thursday, worth thanks
2. **[ð] + [ð]** : bathe there, breathe the fresh air, smooth themselves
3. **[t/d] + [θ/ð]** : opened the door, played the guitar, put that cup, the important thing
4. **[ð] + Vowel** : breathe again, clothe and feed, clothe in black
5. **Miscellaneous** : breathe slowly, miss the chance, pass through, the fifth street, with that, worth that

B. Sentences 244

1. It's nice to breathe in the fresh air in the morning.
2. The problem with this apartment is that it'll be a good 30-minute walk to school.
3. How can I get the best service with the most reasonable rates?
4. The important thing is that you trust them.
5. We crossed the river on a small boat.
6. I wished that I hadn't said such a foolish thing.

Nursery Rhymes 20 245

I saw three ships come sailing by,
Sailing by, sailing by,
I saw three ships come sailing by,
On New Year's Day in the morning.

And what do you think was in them then,
In them then, in them then,
And what do you think was in them then,
On New Year's Day in the morning.

Key Points 8　246

音節 (Syllable) とは

音節とはある母音または二重母音を中心にして，その前後の音がそれに密接に結び付いてまとまりをなす最小の音声単位である*。英語の語 (word) は音節が一つだけの場合と，いくつかの音節が結合して成立している場合とがある。

(1) 単音節語 : do [duː], east [iːst], I [ai], street [striːt]

(2) 二音節語 : chick-en [tʃíkin], cof-fee [kɔ́ːfi], en-joy [endʒɔ́i], mis-take [mistéik]

(3) 多音節語 : com-mu-ni-ca-tion [kəmjùːnəkéiʃən], in-ter-na-tion-al-i-za-tion [ìntərnæʃ(ə)nəlizéiʃ(ə)n], pho-to-graph [fóutə-græ̀f], tech-nol-o-gy [teknɑ́lədʒi]

* 母音単独で音節を構成する場合もある。また，button の n のように syllabic consonant と呼ばれる子音は，単独で音節を構成する（⇒ Key Points 15, P.113）。

Key Points 9　247

子音結合 (Consonant-cluster)

英語の音節構造は日本語と大きく異なり，一つの音節の中で母音を中心として，その片側または両側に子音がいくつか連続して生じたり，単語の末尾が子音だけで終わったりするのが普通である。このように一つの音節の中で子音が連続して生じることを，子音結合と言う。

単音節語の子音結合の例

(1) CV : go, tea
(2) CCV : play, tree
(3) CCCV : screw, spray
(4) VC : eat, ill
(5) VCC : act, old
(6) VCCC : asks, uncle*
(7) CVC : hit, tape
(8) CCVC : drive, glass
(9) CCCVC : screen, strike
(10) CVCC : jump, soft
(11) CVCCC : films, temple*
(12) CCVCC : friend, twelve
(13) CCVCCC : glimpse, prompt
(14) CCCVCC : script, strict
(15) CCCVCCC : scramble*, sprinkle*

*印のついた語は音節子音を含んでいるので二音節語と考えられる。Key Points 15 (P.113) を参照。

* V は母音 (vowel)，C は子音 (consonant) を表わす。

Exercise 15

A. Listen carefully and circle the letter of the words or sentences which are correctly pronounced. 248

1. a) thigh b) thigh c) thy
2. a) either b) ether c) either
3. a) tank b) thank c) tank
4. a) three b) tree c) three
5. a) day b) they c) they
6. a) those b) those c) doze
7. a) I don't like ether.
   b) I don't like either.
   c) I don't like either.
8. a) That's a wonderful team.
   b) That's a wonderful team.
   c) That's a wonderful theme.
9. a) Rabbits breathe quickly.
   b) Rabbits breed quickly.
   c) Rabbits breathe quickly.

B. Listen carefully and fill in the blanks. 249

1. Arthur felt the corners of his (   ) (   ) his (   ).
2. Do you (   ) you can go to the (   ) on (   )?
3. (   ) of my parents was at home when my (   ) came back.
4. I want to (   ) in (   ) fresh sunshine.
5. Her (   ) has been in the hospital for more (   ) (   ) (   ).

Lesson 16

[s]–[z]

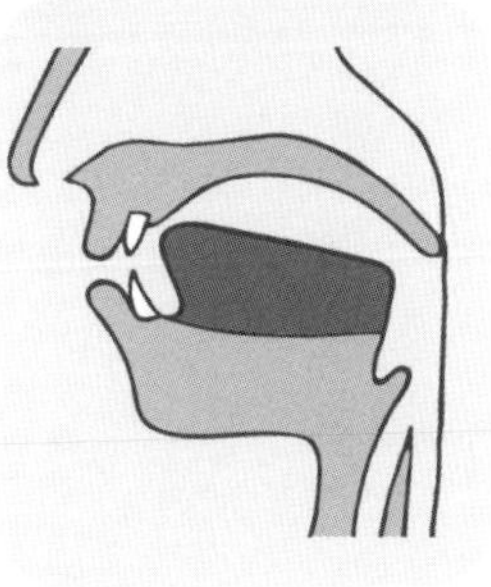

舌先を上歯茎に近づけ，舌と歯のすき間から［ス］と息を強く出して発音する。
[si] [zi] は日本語の「シ」や「ジ」とは異なるので注意。

1 [s] (Voiceless Alveolar Fricative)

A. Words (1) 250

Initial	Medial	Final
city	assist	advice
second	insist	campus
sample	message	famous
science	process	peace
soap	receive	thanks

B. Words (2) 251

homesick, series, silk, single, system, essay, essence, gossip, cycle, scene, scissors, muscle, loose, psalm, psychology, hasten, listen, sword, waltz, axe, accent, accessory, accident ＊黙字 s を含む語
aisle, corps, Illinois, island, Louisville

C. Consonant-clusters 252

Initial	Scotland, slope, smile, sneaker, spoon, sport, steam, stewardess, studio, switch, screen, square, splendid, spring, street, strike
Medial	Australia, basket, discuss, history, instant, system
Final	chopsticks, contents, economics, electronics, ethics, fireworks, mathematics, physics, politics

D. Sentences 253

1. Sister Susan will sing us some sweet Swiss songs.
2. Some passengers on the cruise ship suffered from severe sea-sickness.
3. Mr. Smith sat silent and said not a single word to his sister.

2 [z] (Voiced Alveolar Fricative)

A. Words (1) 254

Initial	Medial	Final
zipper	dessert	quiz
zero	example	freeze
zebra	laser	jazz
zone	puzzle	prize
zoom	thousand	lose

B. Words (2) 255

cousin, houses, Ms., music, possess, disease, raise, bazaar, magazine, pansy, zigzag, zip code, buzzer, buzz, anxiety, examination, xenon, xylophone

C. Consonant-clusters 256

Medial	dismal, Moslem, prism, prison, puzzle
Final	annals, arms, besides, clothes, goods, leaves, lens, needs, knives, remains, selve, teens

D. Sentences 257

1. Rosa went to the bank and deposited 300 dollars in her account.
2. Don't forget to write your zip code on the envelope.
3. My cousin was delighted to see the zebras in the zoo.
4. Now is the most pleasant season in New Zealand.

3 -1. Contrast between [s] and [θ]

A. Words 258

1. sing—thing
2. sick—thick
3. face—faith
4. pass—path
5. use(*n.*)—youth
6. worse—worth

B. Sentences 259

1. Do you think you can repair the sink?
2. The growth of the gross domestic product has been steady.
3. Pass by a moss-covered path, and you'll find the theater.

3 -2. Contrast between [z] and [dz]

(260)

1. as—adds
2. bees—beads
3. cars—cards
4. feels—fields
5. guys—guides
6. holes—holds
7. knees—needs
8. men's—mends
9. rise—rides
10. size—sides

4 Sound Transitions

A. Phrases (261)

1. **[s] + [s]** : Christmas season, ice-skate, mass psychology, Alice Smith, this seat, this sofa, this store, this story
2. **[s] + [ʃ]** : nice shirt, this shop, this show, tennis shoes
3. **[s] + [j]** : bless you, in case you, kiss you, miss you, pass your, this uniform, this year
4. **[z] + [j]** : as usual, as yet, as your, cause you, Ms. Young
5. **[z] + [ʃ]** : his shot, is she, was she, was shot
6. **[s/z] + Vowel** : a glass of, this apple, worse at, blaze up the world, close it, doze off, gaze at, his effort

B. Sentences (262)

1. Pass the oranges, please. I'll make another glass of juice.
2. Put these sandwiches in the basket in case you get hungry.
3. Let me see your new tennis shoes.
4. "Has your father come home yet?" "No, he's still at the gas station."
5. Pizza delivery service is available in this city.
6. This shop will be closed at ten on Wednesdays.
7. Your husband will miss you while you are in Switzerland.
8. This year I suppose we will have a lot of snow, as usual.
9. Did you do it as you were told?
10. What was she doing when you went into her office?

Key Points 10　263

複数形および三単現 -s, -es と所有格の -'s, -s' の発音法

(1) [-iz] ： 単語の語尾が [s, z, ʃ, ʒ, tʃ, dʒ] などの場合

foxes, roses, dishes, garages, matches, bridges, mixes, closes, catches, judges, George's, James's

(2) [-z] ： 語尾が (1) 以外の有声音の場合

cars, cards, flowers, plans, songs, tables, trains, comes, goes, loves, says, tells, Helen's, Linda's

(3) [-s] ： 語尾が (1) 以外の無声音の場合

cakes, cuffs, cups, desks, hats, ropes, students, tapes, gets, helps, speaks, thinks, Jack's, Margaret's

Key Points 11　264

規則動詞の活用語尾 -ed の発音法

(1) [-t] ： 動詞の原形が [t] 以外の無声音で終わる場合

asked, crossed, danced, helped, kissed, laughed, looked, stopped, talked, thanked, walked, wished

(2) [-d] ： 原形が [d] 以外の有声音および母音で終わる場合

arrived, believed, called, enjoyed, judged, listened, lived, loved, mailed, ordered, planned, played

(3) [-id] ： 原形が [t] [d] で終わる場合。ただし形容詞相当語の場合は例外

added, admitted, attended, founded, intended, invited, needed, painted, started, visited, waited, wanted

（例外）blessed [blésid], learned [lə́:rnid], etc.

Key Points 12 265

無声化 (Devocalization)

有声音が隣の無声音の影響で無声化することがある。

Phrases

(1) have [hæv] + to → have to [hǽftə]
(2) has [hæz] + to → has to [hǽstə]
(3) had [hæd] + to → had to [hǽ(t)tə]
(4) of [əv] + course → of course [əfkɔ́ːrs]
(5) used [ju:zd] + to → used to [juːstə]

Sentences

(1) Susan has to meet her manager tomorrow morning.
(2) I have to hand in an assignment by next Tuesday.
(3) You will soon get used to your new surroundings.
(4) Of course he is a nice person.

Nursery Rhymes 21 266

If you sneeze on Monday, you sneeze for danger;
Sneeze on a Tuesday, kiss a stranger;
Sneeze on a Wednesday, sneeze for a letter;
Sneeze on a Thursday, something better;
Sneeze on a Friday, sneeze for sorrow;
Sneeze on a Saturday, see your sweetheart tomorrow;
Sneeze on a Sunday, your safety seek,
Or the devil will take you for the rest of the week.

Exercise 16

A. Listen carefully and circle the letter of the words or sentences which are correctly pronounced.

267

1. a) ice b) eyes c) ice
2. a) sing b) sing c) thing
3. a) breeze b) breathe c) breeze
4. a) zoo b) do c) do
5. a) sell b) sell c) shell
6. a) breeze b) breeds c) breeze
7. a) rose b) rose c) roads
8. a) seeds b) seas c) seeds
9. a) We were studying then. b) We were studying Zen.
   c) We were studying then.
10. a) Do you think it's too thick? b) Do you think it's too thick?
    c) Do you think it's too sick?

B. Listen carefully and fill in the blanks. 268

1. He ( ) ( ) mother looks ( ) ( ) ( ) ( ).
2. I am afraid she ( ) ( ) study ( ) evening.
3. How about another ( ) ( ) beer?
4. Did you buy your ( ) ( ) in ( ) ( )?
5. I ( ) ( ) call Mr. ( ) before ( ).
6. A: How ( ) ( ) holidays?
   B: I had a great time. What about you?
   A: I stayed at home. Did you hear about Kenji?
   B: He left for the ( ) ( ) days ( ) ( ) ( ) exchange student.
   A: Oh, really? I think he will soon ( ) ( ) a lot.

Lesson 17 [ʃ]–[ʒ]

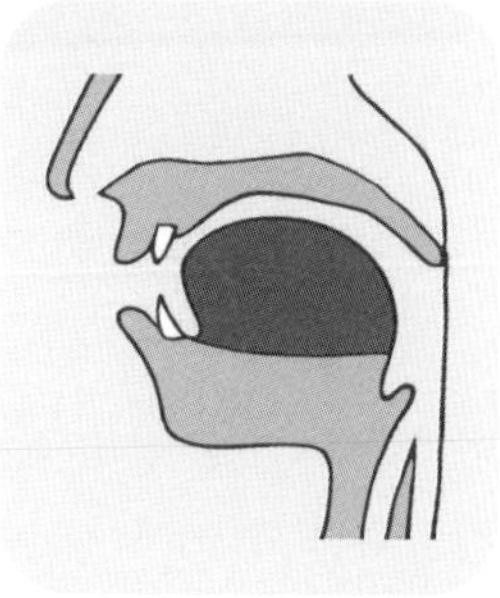

唇をまるめて突き出し，上下の歯の間隔を狭くし，舌先を上歯茎の奥に近づけて，そのすき間から［シ］と息を強く出す。

1 [ʃ] (Voiceless Alveo-palatal Fricative)

A. Words (1) 269

Initial	Medial	Final
ship	delicious	cash
shell	fashion	clash
short	machine	fresh
sugar	mission	punish
shoes	nation	Spanish

B. Words (2) 270

anxious, brochure, chivalry, chandelier, chauffeur, chef, Chicago, conscious, cushion, musician, patient, ratio, Russian, special, Washington

C. Consonant-clusters 271

Initial shriek, shrill, shrimp, shrine, shrink, shrug

D. Sentences 272

1. Shall we make a short trip to Chicago?
2. “Wash the dishes, Sheila,” the chef shouted impatiently.
3. She sat in the shade of a tree looking at the ships.
4. Shirley served us special champagne and a delicious shrimp salad.
5. The shopkeeper showed me a pair of shiny, fashionable shoes.
6. I’m sure I’ll have finished this work by tomorrow.

2 [ʒ] (Voiced Alveo-palatal Fricative)

A. Words (1) 273

Initial	Medial	Final
NONE	confusion	camouflage
—	leisure	garage
—	measure	prestige
—	seizure	rouge
—	usual	sabotage

B. Words (2) 274

casual, Indonesia, luxurious, massage, television

C. Consonant-clusters

No relevant words

D. Sentences 275

1. Shall I measure you?
2. King David saw a vision of the Messiah.
3. Many students spend their leisure time watching television.
4. May I have the pleasure of inviting you to a Parisian show on a showboat?
5. The accidental explosion in the gas station caused shock and confusion.

3 Contrast between [ʃ] and [s]

A. Words 276

1. ship—sip
2. she—sea
3. sheet—seat
4. she'll—seal
5. shin—sin
6. shelf—self
7. shift—sift
8. short—sort
9. shame—same
10. clash—class

B. Sentences 277

1. She sells sea-shells by the seashore.
2. She wants to see the Japan Sea.
3. She'll sell her seal coat.
4. Why don't you put a sheet on the seat?
5. The witness said the box was in the shed.
6. It's a shame to make the same mistake.

4 Sound Transitions

A. Phrases 278

1. **[ʃ] + [ʃ]** : brush shoes, English shirts, fish ships, fresh shrimp, mesh shoes, wash shirts
2. **[ʃ] + Vowel** : British Airways, push over, rush hour

B. Sentences 279

1. I got some fresh shrimp at the fish shop.
2. I have to wash shirts and brush shoes before I leave for my trip tomorrow.
3. British Airways announce the departure of Flight 720 to Paris.
4. Dr. Reischauer left his office at four to avoid the evening rush hour.

Tongue Twister 2 280

She sells sea-shells by the sea shore;

The shells that she sells are sea-shells I'm sure.

So if she sells sea-shells by the sea shore,

I'm sure that the shells are sea-shore shells.

Exercise 17

A. Listen and circle the letter of the words or sentences which are correctly pronounced.

1. a) sheet b) sheet c) seat 281
2. a) sip b) ship c) sip
3. a) scene b) sheen c) scene
4. a) shell b) sell c) sell
5. a) same b) same c) shame
6. a) Who has spoiled this seat?
   b) Who has spoiled this sheet?
   c) Who has spoiled this sheet?
7. a) Why don't you take a ship?
   b) Why don't you take a sip?
   c) Why don't you take a ship?
8. a) Sue is sewing her dress.
   b) Sue is showing her dress.
   c) Sue is sewing her dress.

B. Listen and fill in the blanks. 282

1. Could you (   ) me some (   ) (   )?
2. "How do you spend your (   ) time?"
   "(   ) I watch (   ) in my room."
3. "Would you kindly (   ) me the way to the (   )?"
   "(   ). I'll (   ) you the (   ) cut."
4. "You went (   ), didn't you?"
   "Yes, I bought a (   ) (   ) and (   ) (   )."

Lesson 18 [h]

[h] (Voiceless Glottal Fricative)

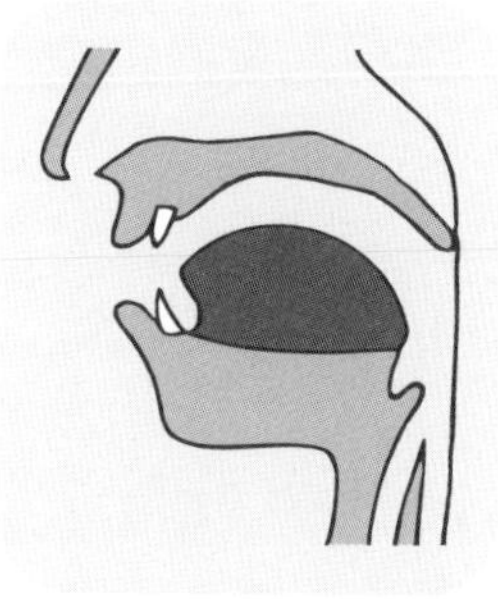

唇と舌は自然のままで，のどの奥から息を強くはき出し，日本語の［ハ，ヘ，ホ］の中の子音と同じ感じで発音する。

A. Words (1) 283

Initial	Medial	Final
heat	ahead	NONE
health	behave	—
heart	behind	—
horse	boyhood	—
who	perhaps	—

B. Words (2) 284

hammer, handle, hello, hook, hood, hotel, humor, rehearsal, vehicle, whole, whom, whose　（注）what, when 等の発音に関しては Key Points (17) を参照。

＊黙字 h を含む語

honest, honor, hour, Ghana, ghost, Graham, rhapsody, rheumatism, rhetoric, rhythm, exhaust, exhibit, shepherd

C. Consonant-clusters 285

Medial　adhere, abhor, Alhambra, childhood, disharmony, inhabit, inhibit, unhappy, unhealthy, uphill

D. Sentences 286

1. Helen used to live in this house with her husband.
2. Henry has hurt his hand with a heavy hammer.
3. How long has Harris been ill? I hope he'll be in good health soon.
4. Heidi, hold your head high.
5. The historic castle is situated high up on a hilltop.

Exercise 18

A. Listen and circle the word or sentence that is correctly pronounced. 287

1. a) heat b) eat
2. a) hill b) ill
3. a) hate b) eight
4. a) hold b) old
5. a) hear b) ear
6. a) hair b) air
7. a) hall b) all
8. a) harm b) arm
9. a) heart b) art
10. a) high b) eye
11. a) Eat up this soup first, Helen.

    b) Heat up this soup first, Helen.
12. a) "Where is my ball?" "It's by the hedge."

    b) "Where is my ball?" "It's by the edge."

B. Listen and fill in the blanks. 288

1. (   ) of the audience in the (   ) clapped for the performer.
2. He suddenly got (   ) on the top of a (   ).
3. It's strange that the people in the village (   ) the number (   ).
4. The (   ) man used to (   ) a pipe between his teeth.
5. You have a good (   ) for (   ) sounds from (   ) (   ).
6. I had a little pony;

   (   ) (   ) was Dapple Gray;
   I (   ) (   ) to a lady,
   To (   ) (   ) (   ) (   );
   She whipped (   ), she lashed (   );
   She drove (   ) (   ) the mire;
   I (   ) not lend my (   ) (   )
   (   ) (   ) the lady's (   ).

Lesson 19 [tʃ]–[dʒ]

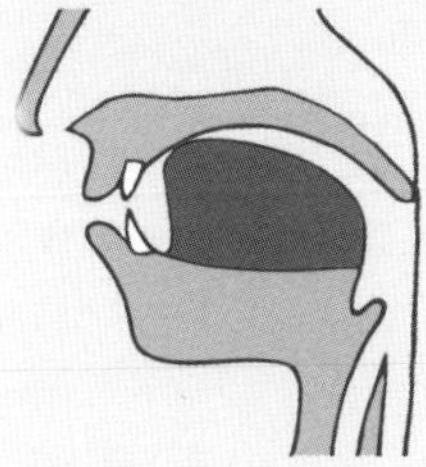

舌先を上歯茎につけ，前舌面を硬口蓋に近づけて，[t]と[ʃ]または[d]と[ʒ]を同時に発音する。日本語の［チ］［ヂ］に近いが，もう少し強く息を出して発音する。

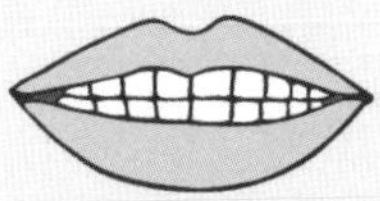

1 [tʃ] (Voiceless Alveo-palatal Affricate)

A. Words (1) 289

Initial	Medial	Final
chicken	fortune	approach
check	future	catch
church	kitchen	each
chalk	nature	March
choose	teacher	touch

B. Words (2) 290

chain, channel, China, butcher, catcher, pitcher, Scotch, Tchaikovsky, Thatcher, creature, suggestion, cello, concerto, Greenwich, sandwich

C. Consonant-clusters 291

Medial	picture, punctual, structure, culture, adventure, century, capture, Christian, mischief, question
Final	bench, branch, French, inch, lunch, pinch

D. Sentences 292

1. Would you teach my child how to play the cello?
2. Charles took his children to church every Sunday.
3. The child tried to catch the chicken in the orchard.
4. Don't you think you're too old for that?
5. Don't count your chickens before they are hatched. 《諺》（とらぬ狸の皮算用）

2 [dʒ] (Voiced Alveo-palatal Affricate)

A. Words (1) 293

Initial	Medial	Final
Jesus	budget	arrange
jealous	magic	college
juice	religion	judge
German	suggest	knowledge
geography	tragedy	marriage

B. Words (2) 294

jewel, major, cabbage, damage, energy, image, refrigerator, badge, lodge, exaggerate, adjective, adjust, grandeur, procedure

C. Consonant-clusters 295

Medial	danger, engine, enjoy, injure, object, soldier
Final	change, indulge, lounge, orange, range, strange

D. Sentences 296

1. Would you rather have cherry juice or orange juice?
2. George enjoyed his package tour to Japan.
3. The community college is near George Bridge.
4. In July they generally enjoy the festival in the village.
5. Janet took a jelly roll and a pack of orange juice out of the refrigerator.

3 -1. Contrast between [tʃ] and [dʒ]

A. Words 297

1. chain—Jane
2. chest—jest
3. cheap—jeep
4. choke—joke
5. choice—Joyce
6. rich—ridge
7. etch—edge
8. larch—large
9. lunch—lunge
10. March—Marge

B. Sentences 298

1. Last year I was looking for a cheap jeep.
2. Jerry was able to overcome binge eating.
3. There is a large larch tree in our backyard.

3 -2. Contrast between [ʒ] and [dʒ]

A. Words 299

1. measure—major
2. pleasure—pledger
3. leisure—ledger
4. version—virgin
5. lesion—legion

B. Sentences 300

1. Josie stays on stage for the whole play.
2. John prepared the ledger at his leisure.
3. They took strong measures against the major unions.

4 Sound Transitions

301

1. **[tʃ] + [tʃ, dʒ, ʃ]** : rich cheese, teach Chinese, which jar, which juice, such shoes, such shows
2. **[dʒ] + [tʃ, dʒ]** : encourage children, exchange chairs, George Johnson, orange juice
3. **stop* + [tʃ]** : ripe cherries, rob chain stores, last chance, old church, quick change, big chance
4. **stop* + [dʒ]** : grape juice, Bob Jones, wet jungle, good Job, pink jacket, dig jewel boxes
5. **[tʃ] + Vowel** : catch it, lunch hour, much oil, which ink

*stop は閉鎖音 [p, b, t, d, k, g] を表わす。

Exercise 19

A. Listen carefully and circle the words that are correctly pronounced in each group. 302

1. a) cherry b) Jerry c) cherry
2. a) March b) March c) Marge
3. a) jeep b) jeep c) cheap
4. a) joke b) choke c) joke
5. a) chain b) chain c) Jane

B. Circle the word that you hear. 303

1. a) choose b) Jews
2. a) lesion b) legion
3. a) leisure b) ledger
4. a) pledger b) pleasure
5. a) version b) virgin
6. a) etch b) edge
7. a) choke b) joke
8. a) ridge b) rich

C. Listen carefully and fill in the blanks. 304

1. ( ) ( ) is for ( ) ( ) Jr.?
2. Shirley gave ( ) ( ) to ( ) ( ).
3. Charlie ( ) some potato ( ) ( ) ( ) and ( ) ( ).
4. The ( ) is approaching the ( ) to ( ) the signal from the ( ).
5. The ( ) ( ) sent from the States hasn't ( ) ( ).
6. I ( ) ( ) a travel agency and ( ) the schedule for my ( ).
7. The rice crop ( ) ( ) is 10 ( ) above the ( ) ( ) ( ) region.

Lesson 20 [r]–[l]

1 [r] (Voiced Alveolar Semivowel/Fricative)

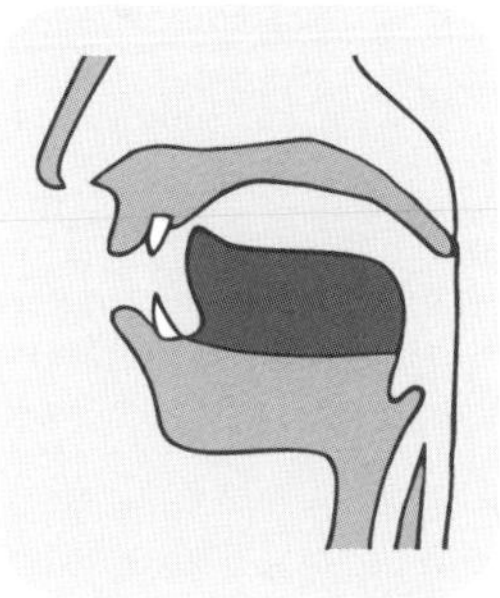

唇を丸く突き出し，舌先を上歯茎の裏に接触しない程度に巻きあげ，口の奥の方にそらせてから強く声を出す。日本語の［ラ］にならないように注意すること。

A. Words (1) 305

Initial	Medial	Final
rich	arrive	beer
regular	borrow	door
right	correct	four
road	mirror	hair
rule	period	tour

B. Words (2) 306

drill, dry, error, organ, radio, rock'n'roll, scrape, straight, carrot, rhyme, rhythm, wrap, wreck, wrist, wrong

C. Review of Consonant-clusters 307

Initial bridge, crowd, dress, France, green, price, screen, shrine, spring, street, throw

Medial address, afraid, agree, apron, attract, cockroach, express, extreme, increase, library, program

D. Retroflex [r]（英音では発音されない［ r ］）308-309

1. **[r] before a consonant** : art, bird, burn, corn, earn, heart, park, person, short, turn, urgent, warm, work
2. **Final [r]** : bar, care, doctor, door, far, fire, guitar, more, occur, pure, star, store, teacher, tower, war

2 [l] (Voiced Alveolar Lateral)

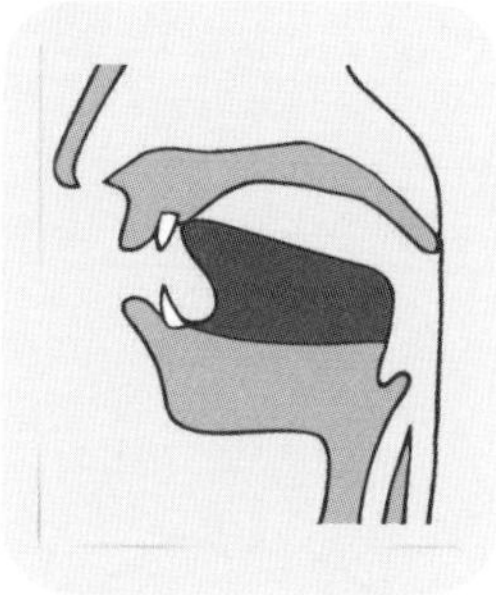

舌先を上歯茎にしっかりと押しつけ，[u]を発音するつもりで舌の両側から声を出す。暗い[l]の場合は舌先が少し後方にずれ，上歯茎に触れないこともある。

A. Words (1) 310

Initial	Medial	Final
leave	allow	until
listen	color	call
learn	collect	mail
long	failure	pearl
lose	million	full

B. Words (2) 311

label, aisle, castle, island, muscle, nestle, whistle, belt, gold, circle, couple, equal, handle, special, table

＊黙字 l を含む語

almond, calf, could, half, Holmes, Lincoln, salmon, should, would

C. Review of Consonant-clusters 312

Initial	blanket, climax, flower, glass, please, slipper
Medial	asleep, English, medley, nobly, pamphlet, ugly

D. Dark [l] ([ɫ]) 313

1. **V* +[l]+C*** : album, building, children, cold, field, film, health, help, illness, milk, self, silver, salt, skillful, told, Wilson, world, yield

2. **Final [l] :** apple, ball, dull, feel, full, girl, grill, people, pool, real, school, tail, tall, tell

*V は母音，C は子音を表わす。

E. Sentences 314

1. Do you know the story of Robinson Crusoe?
2. Taylor Swift has announced her new world tour.
3. These red roses are really very pretty.
4. My brother dropped in a drug store around the street corner.
5. The railroad bridge across the river was rebuilt last April.
6. All is well that ends well.《諺》（終わり良ければすべて良し）
7. I don't feel like listening to the radio any longer.
8. The old man lived a dull life alone in a little bungalow.
9. Lucy was late for class in the chemical lab.
10. Bill fell off the high incline at the top of the hill.

3 Contrast between [r] and [l]

A. Words 315

1. right—light
2. race—lace
3. rate—late
4. rain—lane
5. wrong—long
6. arrive—alive
7. correct—collect
8. grass—glass
9. crime—climb
10. fruit—flute

B. Sentences 316

1. We walked along a lane lined with lilies in the rain.
2. Where is the price list for the wrist watches?
3. Mr. Long took the wrong train at Liverpool.
4. I found a glass doll in the grass.
5. Turn to the right at the next corner. You'll see a traffic light on your right.

Key Points 13 317

clear [l] と dark [l] ([ɫ]) について

　母音や半母音 [j] の前の [l] は舌先を歯茎に押しつけて発音されるので明るく澄んだ感じの [l] (clear [l]) と呼ばれる。（例）life, aloud, million, etc.

一方，子音の前や語尾の [l] は舌の形が [u] の発音に似て暗い音であるので dark [l] ([ɫ]) と呼ばれる。（例）milk, feel, oil

4 Sound Transitions: [r]-linking

A. Phrases 318-319

a pair of, as a matter of, cheer up, far away, father and mother,

for a week, for instance, here and there, more and more,

take care of, there are, there is

B. Sentences 320-321

1. Mother has gone out for a day's shopping.
2. I think I should leave for Osaka now, and thank you for everything.
3. May I take care of your bag?
4. As far as I know, they're unrelated.
5. The rain will stop soon. Let's wait here for a while.
6. Are you in favor of her proposal?
7. Is there enough food for all the guests?

Key Points 14 322-323

(1) Retroflex [r]—そり舌音（反転音）の [r]

米音では子音の前および語尾の r は，舌の反転を一層強くして発音する反転音の [r] となり，半母音的性格のものとなる。しかし英音では子音の前や語尾の r は一般に発音されない。（例）four, work, star, further

(2) 連結現象 (Liaison or Linking)

実際の話し言葉では単語を一つ一つ区切って発音するのではなく，一定のまとまりのある意味グループをあたかも一つの語のように続けて言うのが自然である。

a) [r]-linking 324-325

イギリス英語では一般に語末の [r] は単独では発音されないが，それに続く語が母音で始まると，その母音が直前の [r] と連結して発音される。この現象を [r]-linking と言う。

（例）after all, cheer up, for example, never again

アメリカ英語では，原則的に語末の [r] は単独でも retroflex [r] として発音されるので，次に来る母音と連結して発音される。

b) その他の子音（[m] [n] [t] [d] [k] [p] [l] [z] [v] など）の linking もある。

（例）come in, clean up, first of all, stand up, milk and sugar, stop it,
fill in, because of, give up

Nursery Rhymes 22 326

(a) Row, row, row your boat
Gently down the stream;
Merrily, merrily, merrily, merrily,
Life is but a dream.

(b) There was a little boy and a little girl
Lived in an alley;
Says the little boy to the little girl,
"Shall I oh shall I?"
Says the little girl to the little boy,
"What shall I do?"
Says the little boy to the little girl,
"I will kiss you!"

(c) Mary had a little lamb,
Little lamb, little lamb,
Mary had a little lamb,
Its fleece was white as snow.

And everywhere that Mary went,
Mary went, Mary went,
Everywhere that Mary went,
The lamb was sure to go.

It followed her to school one day,
School one day, school one day,
Followed her to school one day,
Which was against the rule.

It made the children laugh and play,
Laugh and play, laugh and play,
Made the children laugh and play,
To see a lamb at school.

Exercise 20

A. Listen and circle the words or sentences that are correctly pronounced in each group.

327

1. a) read b) read c) lead
2. a) list b) wrist c) wrist
3. a) rest b) lest c) rest
4. a) play b) play c) pray
5. a) cloud b) crowd c) cloud
6. a) glass b) glass c) grass
7. a) That's quite long, isn't it?
   b) That's quite wrong, isn't it?
   c) That's quite long, isn't it?
8. a) A dog was running in the lane.
   b) A dog was running in the rain.
   c) A dog was running in the rain.

B. Listen carefully and fill in the blanks. 328

1. Turn (   ) at the next (   ).
2. The church is not a place to (   ) but to (   ).
3. The teacher is (   ) our papers to (   ) mistakes in our writing.
4. The gate of the (   ) (   ) is closed today, but the door has no (   ).
5. (   ) the package and (   ) (   ) (   ) your (   ).
6. Let's take a (   ) (   ) (   ) while.
7. As a (   ) (   ) fact, the nurse didn't (   ) (   ) (   ) the patient.

Lesson 21

[m]–[n]–[ŋ]

1 [m] (Voiced Bilabial Nasal)

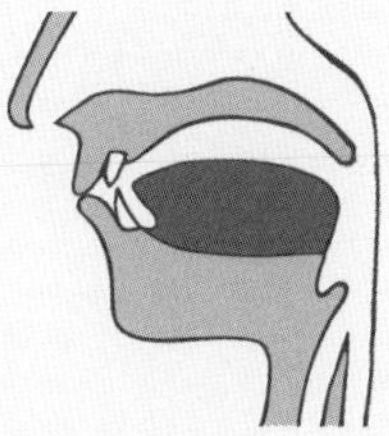

両唇をしっかり閉じて口から息が出ないようにし，［ム］と言うつもりで鼻から声を出す。語末の［ -m ］は両唇を閉じたままで終わるようにする。

A. Words (1) 329

Initial	Medial	Final
meet	famous	dream
member	memory	game
March	remain	dime
moment	summer	warm
move	Thomas	room

B. Words (2) 330

comma, hammer, autumn, column, calm, palm, salmon, climb, comb, lamb, tomb, pump, Mt. McKinley, Mr. McMillan

C. Review of Consonant-clusters 331

Initial	small, smart, smell, smog, smock, smoke, smooth
Medial	member, November, number, remember, symbol, umbrella, comfortable, company, jumper, temperature, trumpet
Final	elm, film, overwhelm, Buddhism, humanism, journalism

D. Sentences 332

1. Please remember me to your family.
2. I can’t imagine what this memo means.
3. The number of temples in Kyoto is tremendous.
4. This movie reminds me of my summer vacation in Rome.

Key Points 15 333

音節子音 (Syllabic consonant) の［ l̩ ］［ m̩ ］［ n̩ ］

音節の核となるのは普通は母音であるが，時には聞こえ度が高く，母音的性格の強い子音 ([l] [m][n]) が音節主音の働きをすることがある。この子音を音節子音と言う。

（例） button, gentle, idol, listen, little, middle, prism, rhythm

2 [n] (Voiced Alveolar Nasal)

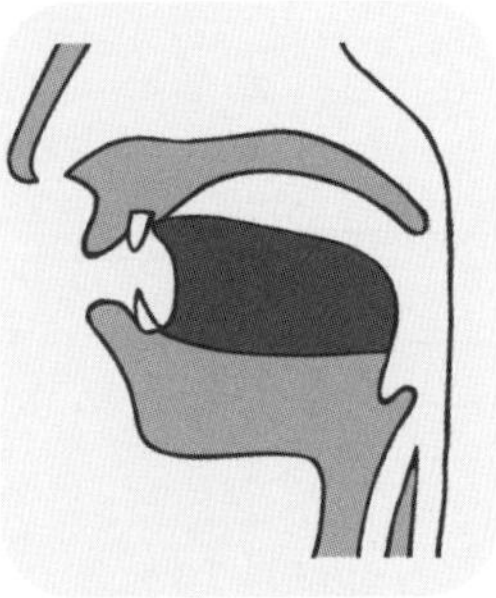

舌先を上歯茎にしっかり押しつけて口から息が出ないようにし，［ヌ］と言うつもりで鼻から声を出す。語尾の [-n] は舌先を上歯茎につけたままで終わるようにする。

A. Words (1) 334

Initial	Medial	Final
need	announce	win
neighbor	enough	none
nice	honest	spoon
nothing	manner	coin
noise	punish	turn

B. Words (2) 335

channel, runner, thinner, tunnel, winner, unknown, unnecessary, Wednesday, knee, knit, knock, pneumonia, Lincoln, campaign, sign

＊黙字 n を含む語

autumn, column, government, hymn, solemn

C. Review of Consonant-clusters 336

Initial	snack, snake, snap, sneeze, snoopy, snow
Medial	answer, central, constant, control, country, dentist, instant, introduce,
Final	friend, kind, ninth, pretend, second

D. Sentences 337

1. Nancy won in the violin competition.
2. Can you play any instruments, Jonathan?
3. Linda's having dinner in an Indonesian restaurant.
4. John's friend Nick is going to buy a secondhand car.
5. I've been here for nine months as an exchange student.

3 [ŋ] (Voiced Velar Nasal)

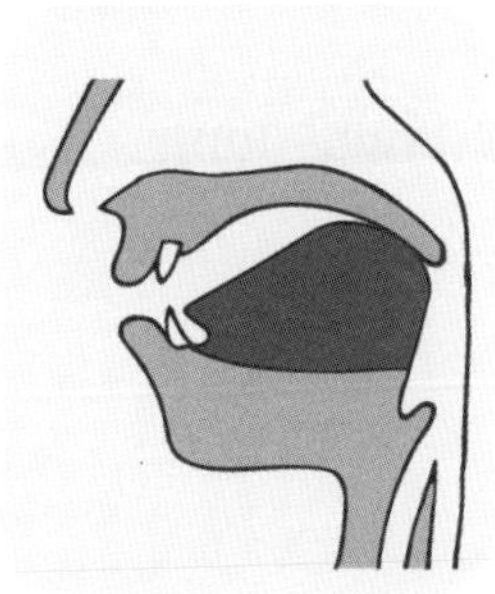

舌の奥（後舌面）を上にあげて軟口蓋につけ，口から息が出ないようにしてから［ン］の音を鼻にひびかせながら発音する。日本語の［グ］の音にならないように注意する。

A. Words (1) 338

Initial	Medial	Final
NONE	hanger	thing
—	ink	slang
—	link	young
—	pink	lung
—	singer	wrong

B. Words (2) [ŋ] と [ŋg] の発音 339

1. [ŋ] : -ng で終わる語末は [ŋ] と発音する。
   among, bring, hang, king, long, sing, tongue, wing

2. [-ŋ-] : 語中で [k] の前にある n は [ŋ] と発音する。
   anchor, anxious, drink, handkerchief, length, monkey, think

3. [-ŋg-] : 語根そのものに含まれている -ng- は [ŋg] と発音する。
   angry, finger, hungry, kangaroo, language, single

4. [-ŋ] : -ng で終わる動詞に -ing や -er がついても [-ŋ] のままで発音する。
   sing—singer—singing, swing—swinger—swinging

5. [-ŋg] : -ng で終わる形容詞に -er, -est がつくと [ŋg] と発音する。
   strong—stronger—strongest, young—younger—youngest

C. Sentences 340

1. Frank is the youngest singer in the choir.
2. I'm going to sing an English song this evening.
3. Did the bee sting your finger?

4 -1. Contrast between [n] and [ŋ]

A. Words 341

1. ran—rang
2. sun—sung
3. thin—thing
4. ton—tongue
5. win—wing
6. kin—king
7. sin—sing
8. clan—clang
9. gone—gong
10. lawn—long

B. Sentences 342

1. A guard ran to the office and rang the alarm bell.
2. Ms. Long sang a song about San Francisco.
3. We sat on a lawn and enjoyed singing for a long time.

4 -2. Contrast between [m] and [n]

A. Words 343

1. game—gain
2. mine—nine
3. more—nor
4. seem—seen
5. sum—sun
6. warm—warn

B. Sentences 344

1. The manager is taking a nap in front of the computer.
2. Did you see Jimmy or Ginny in the morning?

Nursery Rhymes 23 345

Sing a song of sixpence,
A pocket full of rye,
Four and twenty blackbirds
Baked in a pie;
When the pie was opened,
The birds began to sing;
Wasn't that a dainty dish
  to set before a king?

The king was in the counting house,
Counting out his money,
The queen was in the parlour,
Eating bread and honey,
The maid was in the garden,
Hanging out the clothes,
When along came a blackbird
  and pecked off her nose.

5 Sound Transitions: [n, m, ŋ]-linking

A. Phrases 346

1. **[n]-linking** : an egg, an honest man, an apple, in all, in an hour,
   in English, in order, men and women, none of us,
   one or two, run away, the Son of God, turn over
2. **[m]-linking** : come on, name and address, some of them, time and money
3. **[ŋ]-linking** : bring about, king and queen, looking at,
   strong and brave, thinking of, young and old
4. **[m] + [m]** : homemade cake, perform magic, some milk, some more

B. Sentences 347

1. Could you make an after-dinner speech in English?
2. Don't forget to write your name and address here.
3. I want to get some money to buy a camera.
4. Bring me a cup of tea, please.
5. Would you like some more coffee?

Key Points 16 348

同化現象 (Assimilation)

子音の Sound Transitions の項ですでに取り扱ってきたが，隣接する 2 つの音の一方が他の影響を受けて，それと全く同じ音かまたは似かよった別の音に変化する現象を同化現象という。

同化には south + ern → southern [sʌ́ðərn] のように，広く一般に用いられて標準音となった確立同化と，発話のスピードやスタイルに関連して起こる偶発同化とがある。偶発同化は日常会話などのくだけた英語の発音で起こることが多い。

(例) as yet [æʒét], did you [didʒu], don't you [dountʃúː], has to [hæstə],
one man [wʌ́mmæn], ten minutes [témminits]

Exercise 21

A. Listen and circle the words or sentences that are correctly pronounced in each group.

1.	a) rang	b) ran	c) rang	349
2.	a) ban	b) bang	c) ban	
3.	a) lawn	b) long	c) lawn	
4.	a) win	b) wing	c) wing	
5.	a) fan	b) fan	c) fang	
6.	a) clan	b) clang	c) clam	
7.	a) ding	b) dim	c) din	
8.	a) Kim	b) kin	c) king	
9.	a) sin	b) Sim	c) sing	
10.	a) some	b) sung	c) sun	

11. a) I didn't know it was wrong.
    b) I didn't know it was wrong.
    c) I didn't know it was Ron.

12. a) Ms. Young had a strange pang.
    b) Ms. Young had a strange pan.
    c) Ms. Young had a strange pang.

B. Listen carefully and fill in the blanks. 350

Jane stood at the door (   ). She (   ) the
(   ) would be here any (   ). Suddenly she saw the
(   ) truck drive up to her (   ) (   ). (   )
(   ) have a letter (   ) (   ) boy friend in Japan?
The (   ) (   ) (   ) the stairs and (   )
as he (   ) (   ) a letter with a Japanese (   )
(   ) (   ). Jane was so excited that she (   ) forgot to
say "Thank you." The mailman (   ) (   ). "I was (   )
once, too," he said to (   ).

Lesson 22 [w]–[j]

1 [w] (Voiced Bilabial Semivowel)

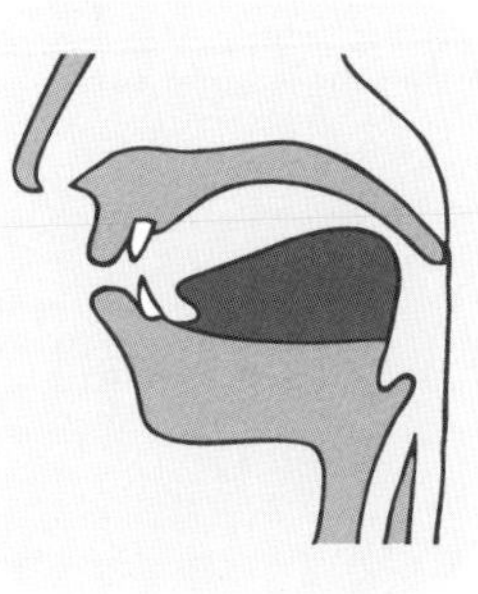

日本語の［ウ］よりも唇をもっと強く前へ突き出してから，短く［ウ］と発音し，次の母音に続ける。日本語にない［wi, wu, we, wɔ］には注意すること。

A. Words (1) 351

Initial	Medial	Final
winter	away	NONE
west	aware	—
work	Hawaii	—
wonder	reward	—
wool	rewind	—

B. Words (2) 352

wet, weight, window, women, wood, between, swim, swing, sweater, twin, quarter, queen, equal, liquid, one, choir, language, suite ＊黙字 w を含む語
wrap, wrist, write, wrong, answer, Greenwich, sword, two

C. Review of Consonant-clusters 353

Initial	dwell, quality, queen, quick, squeeze, squirrel, sweater, swim, Swiss, tweed, twelve, twilight
Medial	always, banquet, between, conquest, distinguish, equal, language, liquid, persuade, penguin

D. Sentences 354

1. I want to buy a warm wool sweater this winter.
2. Mr. Wordsworth, we would like to make a request.
3. Why don't you wait one more week?
4. Professor Walters' interview questions are always quite stimulating.
5. What is worth doing at all is worth doing well. 《諺》（やる以上は立派にやれ）

Key Points 17

355-356

語頭の wh- の発音について

(1) [w] の脱音化で [h-] と発音する場合

who [huː], whole [houl], whose [huːz], whom [huːm]

(2) [hw-]([ʍ]) と発音する場合

標準南部イギリス英語では以下のような wh- の語でも [hw-] と発音せず，[w-] と発音することが多いが（wine-whine merger と呼ばれる h が脱落する現象)，アメリカ英語では地域や年齢により [hw-] と発音される場合もある。

	what	**when**	**where**	**which**	**why**
[hw-]	[hwat]	[hwen]	[hwɛər]	[hwitʃ]	[hwai] [wai]
[w-]	[wat]	[wen]	[wɛə]	[witʃ]	[wai]

	wheel	**white**	**whether**	**while**	**whiskey**
[hw-]	[hwiː1]	[hwait]	[hwéðər]	[hwail]	[hwiski]
[w-]	[wiː1]	[wait]	[wéðə]	[wail]	[wiski]

従って，wh- を [w-] ではなく [hw-] で発音する場合は，次のような 2 語は発音が異なり，意味上の対立がある。

Contrast between [hw] and [w]

1. whether — weather
2. which — witch
3. where — wear
4. why — Y
5. wheel — we'll

Nursery Rhymes 24

357

"Where are you going, my pretty maid?"
"I am going a-milking, sir," she said.

"May I go with you, my pretty maid?"
"You're kindly welcome, sir," she said.

"What is your father, my pretty maid?"
"My father's a farmer, sir," she said.

"What is your fortune, my pretty maid?"
"My face is my fortune, sir," she said.

"Then I can't marry you, my pretty maid!"
"Nobody asked you, sir!" she said.

2 [j] (Voiced Alveo-palatal Semivowel)

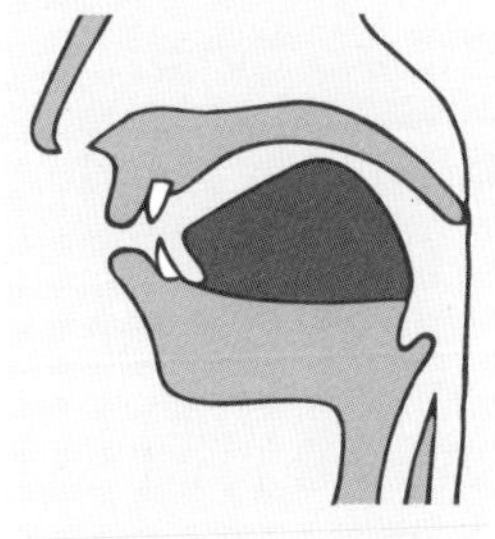

舌先を下の前歯の裏に軽く触れさせ，舌の中央部を上にもちあげ，力を入れて強く［イ］と発音する。日本語の［ヤ］［ユ］［ヨ］の子音部に近い音であるが，それよりも強く鋭く発音する。

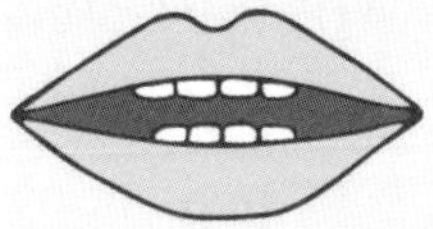

A. Words (1) 358

Initial	Medial	Final
year	amuse	NONE
yellow	familiar	—
young	lawyer	—
yacht	opinion	—
use	peculiar	—

B. Words (2) 359

uniform, union, university, Europe, humor, beauty, cue, queue, security, feudalism, few, nephew, value, behavior, failure, senior, Italian, million, onion, William, yen, yes, yesterday, hallelujah

C. Sentences 360

1. My music teacher goes to New York every year.
2. My beautician has a cute white terrier.
3. Your younger brother is at Yale, isn't he?
4. Do you know how to use yeast when you bake bread?
5. There is a long queue in front of the university museum.

Nursery Rhymes 25 361

Wee Willie Winkie runs through the town
Upstairs and downstairs in his night-gown,
Rapping at the window, crying through the lock,
Are the children all in bed, for it's now eight o'clock?

Key Points 18 362

[juː] と [uː] の発音について

[uː] の前に [j] がつく時とつかない時とがあるが，原則的には次のようになっている。

(1) [juː] と発音する場合……閉鎖音([p] [b] [k] [g])，鼻音([m])，摩擦音([f] [v] [h])の後およびアクセントのある母音 + [l] の後では [juː] と発音される。

pupil, beaty, cue, argue, music, few, view, human, value, volume

(2) [juː] と [uː] の両方の発音がある場合……[t] [d] [n] [s] [z] の後では [juː] と [uː] の両方の発音があるが，アメリカ英語では [j] が脱落し，[uː] と発音される傾向がある（yod-dropping と呼ばれる）。363-364

stew, student, stupid, studio, stewardess, due, dew, duty, endure, knew, neutral, new, newspaper, Newsweek, nuclear

特に [s] [z] の後やアクセントのない短母音 + [l] の後では [uː] と発音されている。

365-366

assume, consume, consumer, pursue, resume, sue, suit, suitable, suicide, illusion, pollute, pollution, salute

Nursery Rhymes 26 367

OVER THE HILLS
AND FAR AWAY

Tom he was a piper's son,

He learnt to play when he was young;

But all the tune that he could play

Was "Over the hills and far away."

Over the hills and a great way off,

The wind shall blow my top-knot off.

3 Contrast between [w] and [r], etc.

A. Words

3-1. Contrast between [w] and [r]

368

1. wait—rate
2. way—ray
3. went—rent
4. west—rest
5. wing—ring
6. wide—ride
7. witch—rich
8. wise—rise

3-2. Contrast between [w] and [ø]*

369

1. woke—oak
2. wear—air
3. queen—keen
4. wall—all
5. sward—sword
6. sweet—seat
7. square—scare
8. swoop—soup

3-3. Contrast between [j] and [ø]*

370

1. yes—S
2. yen—N
3. Yale—ale
4. yeast—east
5. yearn—earn
6. year—ear
7. feud—food
8. pure—poor

B. Sentences

371

1. You aren't accustomed to eating Western food, are you?
2. Their serious problem is living wages for the aged.
3. I don't know whether we'll have good weather next Sunday.
4. Why did she write a letter 'I' with her lipstick?
5. Last year I often had earaches.
6. How many l's are there in 'yell'?

*[ø] は当該の音を含まないことを表す。

Exercise 22 372

A. Listen and circle the words or sentences that are correctly pronounced in each group.

1.	a) wipe	b) ripe	c) wipe	7.	a) ax	b) wax	c) wax
2.	a) rate	b) rate	c) wait	8.	a) earth	b) worth	c) earth
3.	a) wing	b) ring	c) wing	9.	a) ear	b) year	c) year
4.	a) racks	b) wax	c) wax	10.	a) yeast	b) east	c) yeast
5.	a) wheat	b) eat	c) wheat	11.	a) ale	b) Yale	c) Yale
6.	a) eye	b) eye	c) why	12.	a) poor	b) pure	c) pure

13. a) Where did you get such a big eel?
    b) Where did you get such a big wheel?
    c) Where did you get such a big eel?
14. a) Don't you know where my ax is?
    b) Don't you know where my wax is?
    c) Don't you know where my wax is?
15. a) Who's going to make the next speech?
    b) Hugh's going to make the next speech.
    c) Who's going to make the next speech?

B. Listen carefully and fill in the blanks. 373

1. The Tigers were (   ) in the seventh (   ).
2. Which do you usually (   ), rye or (   )?
3. (   ) have you got a black (   ).
4. The (   ) around here is (   ) 500,000 yen for a square meter.
5. I had to (   ) to hear the exchange (   ).
6. Can you (   ) the lawn a little (   ) in the afternoon?

Key Points 19

脱落現象 (Elision)

Sound Transitions ですでに扱っているように，自然に話されることばの流れの中では，隣接する 2 つの子音が同じ音か，その調音位置や調音の仕方が似ているため，前の子音が発音されずに脱落することがある。これを子音の脱落という。

A. Phrases 374

1. **[p] の脱落** : deep dish, keep goats, keep pace, sleep peacefully, stop talking, top boots
2. **[t] の脱落** : don't mind, first chance, first stop, hot tea, last night, reached Tokyo, sit down
3. **[d] の脱落** : good driver, good-bye, grabbed them, kind nurse, loud cry, old man, road test, sound good
4. **[k] の脱落** : back door, book-keeping, dark clouds, take care
5. **[g] の脱落** : Big Ben, big car, big dog, big game
6. **[f] の脱落** : enough food, half finished, rough voice
7. **[s] の脱落** : less sugar, tennis shoes, this seat, this store, walks slowy
8. **その他の子音** :
   - **[b]** ebb tide, rob banks
   - **[tʃ]** rich children, which judge
   - **[n]** can never, can not
   - **[ʃ]** brush shoes, fresh shrimp
   - **[m]** homemade, some money

B. Sentences 375

1. Do you know the lady who is having lunch at the next table?
2. You've caught a cold. Take good care of yourself.
3. I want to meet you at ten tomorrow morning.
4. Why don't you sit down and have some homemade cookies?
5. I found some nice tennis shoes in this shop.

FAIRY TALES
COSMOS
encyclopedia
POEMS
dino
ABC
12
BIRDS
princess
ATLAS
ADVENTURE

CHAPTER II

STRESS & INTONATION

FAIRY TALES
COSMOS
encyclopedia
POEMS
dino
ABC
12
BIRDS
princess
ATLAS
ADVENTURE

I STRESS PATTERNS

1 Word Stress

(1) 個々の単語のストレス（アクセント）

英語の二音節以上の単語には強勢が置かれる音節 (Stressed or Accented Syllable) がある。下の単語の最も強く発音する音節にストレス記号 (´) を付けたあとで音声を開き，発音しなさい。

376

1. accurate
2. advantage
3. ancestor
4. antique
5. atmosphere
6. biography
7. character
8. comfortable
9. concentrate
10. consequence
11. contribute
12. convenient
13. correspond
14. distribute
15. educate
16. electricity
17. engineer
18. equal
19. execute
20. genuine
21. influence
22. instrument
23. interrupt
24. linguistics
25. mathematics
26. mischievous
27. percentage
28. prejudice
29. realism
30. recommend
31. separate
32. volunteer

(2) 派生語における強勢の位置の移動

Compare the stress pattern in the following pairs.

377

1. commúnicate—communicátion
2. cúrious—curiósity
3. cólony—colónial
4. démonstrate—demonstrátion
5. énergy—energétic
6. démocrat—demócracy—democrátic—demócratize—democratizátion
7. ecónomy—económic(al)—económics—ecónomist—ecónomize—economizátion
8. phótograph—photógrapher—photógraphy—photográphic

(3) 品詞による強勢の差異

378

	(a) Noun or Adjective	(b) Verb
	ˊ ˋ	ˋ ˊ
1.	conduct [kɑ́ndə̀kt]	conduct [kə̀ndʌ́kt]
2.	conflict [kɑ́nflìkt]	conflict [kə̀nflíkt]
3.	content	content
4.	convict	convict
5.	desert [dézə̀rt]	desert [dìzə́rt]
6.	digest	digest
7.	increase	increase
8.	insult	insult
9.	object	object
10.	present [préznt]	present [prìzént]
11.	produce	produce
12.	progress	progress
13.	protest [próutèst]	protest [prə̀tést]
14.	record [rékə̀rd]	record [rìkɔ́ərd]
15.	subject	subject
16.	survey	survey

Exceptions

ˊ ˋ	ˊ ˋ (or ˊ ˊ)
export	export
import	import

強勢の位置が移動する場合には，一般に母音の質的な変化を伴うことがある。
ˊは最も強く発音される第一アクセントの位置を表し，ˋは次に強く発音される第二アクセントの位置を表している。

Exercise 23 379

Listen to the audio and put stress marks over the underlined words. Then read the sentences aloud.

1. A guide will conduct you through the British Museum.
2. There are some big deserts in the U.S.A.
3. All the students object to the new plan.
4. There was a rapid increase in population.
5. We can't convert a man by insult.
6. John will present her with some jewels.
7. They won't permit you to enter the room.
8. According to the newspaper, the suspect is still at large.
9. Some fats digest easily, some don't.
10. The students waited in perfect silence.

380

2 Stress in Word Combinations

(1) Adjective + Noun and Compound words

(a) Adjective + Noun	(b) Compound words
ˊ— ˊ—	ˊ— ˋ—
bláck bírd（黒い鳥）	bláckbìrd（クロウタドリ）
bláck bóard（黒い板）	bláckbòard（黒板）
blúe prínt	blúeprìnt（青写真）
blúe béll	blúebèll（ヒヤシンス）
bríef cáse（簡単な事件）	bríefcàse（折りかばん）
bríck yárd（煉瓦を敷いた中庭）	bríckyàrd（煉瓦工場）
cótton bélt	Cótton Bèlt（米国綿花地帯）
críminal láwyer（罪を犯した弁護士）	críminal làwyer（刑事問題専門弁護士）
króss wórd（意地悪なことば）	crósswòrd（クロスワード）
dárk róom（暗い部屋）	dárkròom（暗室）
Énglish téacher（英国人の先生）	Énglish tèacher（英語の先生）
gréen bélt	gréen bèlt（緑地帯）
hígh wáy	híghwày（高速道路）
hót pláte（熱い皿）	hót plàte（ホットプレート・料理用鉄板）
líght hóuse	líghthòuse（灯台）
nóble mán	nóblemàn（貴族）
shórt hánd	shórthànd（速記）
Spánish stúdent（スペイン人の学生）	Spánish stùdent（スペイン語を勉強している学生）
stróng bóx	stróngbòx（金庫）

whíte hóuse	Whíte Hòuse（米国大統領官邸）
cómic bóok sàlesman （こっけいな人柄の本のセールスマン）	cómic bòok sálesman （漫画本のセールスマン）
óld stámp collèctor（年輩の切手収集家）	óld stàmp colléctor（古い切手の収集家）
líght hóuse kèeper（体重の軽い家政婦）	líghthòuse kéeper（灯台守）

Exercise 24 381

Put stress marks over the underlined words and word combinations.

1. A blackboard isn't always a black board. It's sometimes green or even white.
2. Our English teacher, Mr. Tanaka is not an English teacher.
3. My uncle lives in a white house, not in the White House!
4. Ms. Right is a lighthouse keeper, not a light house keeper.

(2) -ing + Noun (Gerund or Present Participle + Noun) 382

(a) Gerund+ Noun 動名詞	(b) Present Participle + Noun 現在分詞
dáncing tèacher（踊りの先生）	dàncing téacher（踊っている先生） (= teacher who is dancing)
díning ròom（食堂）	dìning lády（食事をしている婦人）
húnting dòg（猟犬）	hùnting dóg（獲物を追いかけている犬）
sléeping càr（寝台車）	slèeping báby（眠っている赤ん坊）
smóking ròom（喫煙室）	smòking cigár（煙っている葉巻）
díning càr（食堂車）	bùrning cár（燃えている車）
físhing vìllage（漁村）	fìshing bírd（魚を捕っている鳥）
júmping ròpe（縄跳びの縄）	jùmping bóy（ジャンプしている少年）
rúnning shòes（ランニングシューズ）	rùnning gírl（走っている少女）
wáiting ròom（待合室）	wàiting cústomer（順番待ちの客）
swímming pòol（水泳プール）	swìmming físh（泳いでいる魚）

Key Points 20

383

-ing + Noun の区別について

-ing の前に for を置いてみて，意味が通じれば，動名詞であり，そうでなければ現在分詞である。

例 (A) a smóking ròom = a room for smoking
　 (B) a sìnking bóat ≠ a boat for sinking

(A) の場合は上のように置き換えられ「喫煙室」という意味であり，smoking にストレスをおく。

(B) の場合は a boat that is sinking と書き換えられ「沈みゆく舟」という意味であり，boat にストレスをおいて強く発音する。

Key Points 21

384

内部連接 (Internal juncture) の型による意味の弁別

(1) 内部閉鎖連接 : 語内における音素と音素のつながり方　例 a name
(2) 内部開放連接 : 語と語の境界におけるつながり方　例 an aim

1. (winter day / win today)
2. (ice cream / I scream)
3. (gray train / great rain)
4. (that stuff / that’s tough)
5. (a name / an aim)
6. (a nail / an ale)
7. (a note / an oat)
8. (a nice drink / an ice drink)
9. (alight / a light)
10. (arose / a rose)
11. (scolder / scold her)
12. (already / all ready)

Exercise 25 385

Put stress marks over the underlined word combinations.

1. The sleeping baby isn't in the sleeping bag.
2. The gentleman who is carrying a walking stick is called a walking dictionary.
3. I'm looking for my knitting needles.
4. The reading room is on the first floor.

Exercise 26 386

Listen and circle either a) or b).（問題用に合成語も意図的に離し，大文字も小文字のままで書いてある部分もあります）

1. The dancing teacher over there is Ms. Johnson.

   a) 踊りの先生　　b) 踊っている先生

2. Did you see a gold fish in his house?

   a) 金魚　　b) 金製の飾り物の魚

3. Jack is a fine clerk.

   a) 優秀な店員　　b) 罰金徴収係

4. He is my German teacher.

   a) ドイツ語の先生　　b) ドイツ人の先生

5. Dr. Casey is our head doctor.

   a) 医長　　b) 精神科医

6. Do you know what cotton belt means?

   a) 米国綿花地帯　　b) 木綿地のベルト

7. Have you seen a black bird around here?

   a) クロウタドリ　　b) 黒い鳥

8. She is a criminal lawyer.

   a) 罪を犯した弁護士　　b) 刑事問題専門の弁護士

9. Mr. Wilson is an old stamp collector.

   a) 年輩の切手収集家　　b) 古切手収集家

10. I know that swimming coach.

a) 泳いでいるコーチ　　b) 水泳のコーチ

11. He is a new car salesman.

a) 新車のセールスマン　　b) 新人の自動車セールスマン

12. He respects his grand father.

a) 偉大な父親　　b) 祖父

13. Put the hot plate on the table.

a) ホットプレート　　b) 熱い皿

14. I like blue bells very much.

a) ヒヤシンス　　b) 青いベル

15. Look at the racing yacht.

a) 競走中のヨット　　b) 競争用のヨット

16. She is an Italian student.

a) イタリア人の学生　　b) イタリア語を勉強している学生

17. A safe is also called a strong box.

a) 金庫　　b) 頑丈な箱

18. My younger brother has been suffering from growing pains.

a) 成長痛　　b) ひどくなっていく痛み

19. Would you like some cold cream?

a) 冷たいクリーム　　b) コールドクリーム
＊クレンジングや洗顔用のクリーム

20. He belongs to a debating team at college.

a) 討論部　　b) 論争中のクラブ

(3) Shift of Stress by Contrast or Rhythm in Sentences and Word Combinations.

387

a) The new student is Jàpanése.

That's not a Chìnése lantern. It's Jápanèse.

b) He's a wéll-knòwn violinist.

His accompanist is also wéll-knówn all over the world.

c) The fóurtèen girls are all fòurtéen.

d) Naturally, the dównstàirs rooms are dòwnstáirs.

388

3 Sentence Stress and Rhythm

(1) Sentence Stress: センテンスの中でストレスのある単語

Content words and Function words（内容語と機能語）について：

一般的に，内容語にはストレスが置かれ，機能語にはストレスが置かれない。

A. Content words（内容語）

1) Noun〔名詞〕
2) Verb〔動詞〕(except *be*, *have* and Auxiliary Verbs listed below in **Function words 3**)
3) Adjective〔形容詞〕
4) Adverb〔副詞〕
5) Demonstrative〔指示詞〕(*this, that, these, those*)
6) Interrogative〔疑問詞〕(*who, when, why*, etc.)
7) Interjection〔間投詞〕(*oh!*, *Hey!*, etc.)

B. Function words（機能語）

1) Article〔冠詞〕(*a, an, the*)
2) Preposition〔前置詞〕(*at, in, of, to,* etc.)
3) Auxiliary Verb〔助動詞〕
   (*be, have, do, will, would, shall, should, can, could, may, might, must*)
4) Personal Pronoun〔人称代名詞〕(*I, my, me, you, your, yours, he, she, it,* etc.)
5) Relative Pronoun〔関係代名詞〕(*who, that, which,* etc.)
6) Relative Adverb〔関係副詞〕(*where, when, why, as,* etc.)
7) Conjunction〔接続詞〕(*and, but, that, as, if,* etc.)
8) "One" used as a pronoun〔代名詞としての one〕
   (例 the green dress and the yellow *one*)

Key Points 22

389

1. 二語の phrasal verb（句動詞）のストレスの位置

動詞には普通センテンス・ストレスが置かれるが，動詞と副詞とからなる二語の動詞の場合は，ストレスが置かれるのは動詞ではなくて副詞である。

例 put ón, split úp, shut úp, put óff, put úp, look óut, pull óut, dig óut

2. 動詞 + 副詞の句動詞と動詞 + 前置詞の句動詞の見分け方

例えば to put on（動詞 + 副詞）と to look at（動詞 + 前置詞）の違いは，次の二通りの方法で見分けられる。

A. 代名詞にして二語の間に入れて見分ける方法

(1) I want to put on that hat → I want to put it on. (○)

(2) I want to look at that picture → I want to look it at. (×)

このような場合，(1) の動詞 + 副詞では put と on の間に it を入れて用いるが，(2) の動詞 + 前置詞句の look at では，look と at の間に it を入れることはできない。

B. What で始まる疑問文で見分ける方法

(1) What are you putting on? → On what are you putting? (×)

(2) What are you looking at? → At what are you looking? (○)

このような場合，(1) では put と on を分けると意味をなさなくなる。

Key Points 23

390

E メールやソーシャルメディア（SNS）などのくだけた英語では文頭の人称代名詞やそれに続く助動詞の省略が見られることがある。

例 (I) Hope you're doing well.

(I have) Just arrived in NYC!

(I will) Go to Tokyo next Friday.

(2) Rhythm

391

英語のリズムの特質は強勢音節の規則的な繰り返しにあり，原則的には強勢と強勢との間はその間にある音節の数の多少にかかわらず時間的にはほぼ等間隔で発音される。そのため，強音勢に挟まれて現われる弱音勢の部分は，その数が増えれば増えるほど，速く弱く不明瞭に曖昧母音 [ə], [i] を用いて発音される。

たとえば，次のような文は，a) b) c) のどの文も同じ音節に同じ強さが置かれ，どの文もほぼ同じリズムで読まれる。これは強勢がおかれない音節が無意識のうちに，速く弱く圧縮されて読まれるからで，これによって英語らしいリズムが生じる。日本人の英語学習者は一つ一つの音節を区切ってポツポツと発音しがちであるから，この英語特有のリズムに馴れる必要がある。

Ex. a) Júdy's a téacher.（1 秒）
　　b) Júdy's a good téacher.（1 秒）
　　c) Júdy's a very good téacher.（1 秒）

Rhythm　練習：Listen and repeat.

(1) a) My fáther gáve my bróther a cár.
　　b) My fáther gáve my little bróther a cár.
　　c) My fáther gáve my little bróther a new cár.
　　d) My fáther gáve my little bróther a new toy cár.

(2) a) Bóys réad bóoks.
　　b) The bóys will réad bóoks.
　　c) The bóys will réad some bóoks.
　　d) The bóys will be réading some bóoks.
　　e) The bóys will be réading some of their bóoks.

英語が「強勢リズムの言語」(stress-timed language) と言われ，上例のように強勢のある音節が規則的に現われるのに対し，日本語は「音節リズムの言語」(syllable-timed language) とされており，すべての音節が等間隔的に現われる。すなわち，日本語では一つ一つの音節（正確にはモーラ = 拍）にほぼ同じ時間をかけて発話するので，音節が増えれば増えるほど時間がかかることになる。

例えば，1. かれ　は　いま　えいご　の　ほん　を　よんで　います。(18 音節）は，
　　　　2. かれ　は　ここに　います。(9 音節）よりほぼ 2 倍の時間がかかることになる。

なお，ここでは散文のリズム練習を取り扱っているが，詩ではリズムは散文以上に重要な要素であり，音節の強弱を単位として規則正しく繰り返される。本書には数多く詩やナーサリーライムを取り上げているので，これらを暗誦して英語のリズム感を身につけてほしい。

(3) Strong form and Weak form

392

日本人の英語学習者はどの音も同じ強さで発音する傾向があるので，英語らしく聞こえるように話すためには，特に Weak form（弱形）の発音に注意する必要がある。

以下は，強形と弱形を持つ例である。意図的に強勢が置かれる場合を除き，通常は弱形で発音される。

強形と弱形の練習：Listen and repeat.

1. a	[ei]	a) She is an A-plus student.
	[ə]	b) This is a car.
2. an	[æn]	a) An orange will do.
	[ən]	b) She has an apple.
3. and	[ænd]	a) A: Is Mary coming alone? B: No, Mary and Amy are coming.
	[ənd]	b) No, but Ruth has answered, and she says she's bringing her boyfriend.
	[ən]	c) Yes, Judy and Meg are both coming.
	[n]	d) Yes, Ed and Bob said they'd come.
		e) bread and butter; boys and girls
4. are	[ɑːr]	a) She's not going, but she says you are.
	[ən]	b) Who are you coming with?
5. as	[æz]	a) Who are you as tall as?
	[əz]	b) I'm as tall as Mike.
6. at	[æt]	a) What's she looking at?
	[ət]	b) I'll see you at the station.
7. but	[bʌt]	a) But, you see, there is a difference.
	[bət]	b) He is rich but unhappy.
8. can	[kæn]	a) I hope you can.
	[kən]	b) I'm sure you can do it.
9. could	[kud]	a) I'd rather ride with you, if I could.
	[kəd]	b) I wish you could have stayed a little longer.

10.	for	[fɔər]	a) Who is he voting for?
		[fər]	b) He's voting for his uncle.
11.	from	[frʌm]	a) Where are you from?
		[frəm]	b) I'm from New York.
12.	has	[hæz]	a) John hasn't gone, has he?
		[həz]	b) Has John left yet?
		[əz]	c) Jerry has just left.
		[z]	d) Cathy's already left.
13.	have	[hæv]	a) "Have I met him?" "Yes, you have."
		[həv]	b) Have you seen it?
		[əv]	c) The teachers have seen it.
		[v]	d) I've seen it.
14.	he	[hiː]	a) He's the one who broke the window.
		[iː]	b) Does he play the piano?
15.	her	[həːr]	a) Give it to her, not him.
		[hər]	b) Her children are sleeping.
		[ər]	c) She's lost her purse.
16.	his	[hiz]	a) It's his book, not hers.
		[iz]	b) What's his name?
17.	him	[him]	a) We gave it to him and his wife.
		[im]	b) I met him at three.
18.	in	[in]	a) Did he put the car in?
		[n]	b) Then he went in the house.
19.	is	[iz]	a) I don't know where she is.
		[z]	b) She's coming.
		[s]	c) It's cooler today than yesterday.

20. not [nɑt] a) True? I think not.
[nt] b) It isn't true.

21. of [ʌv] a) What's this table made of?
[əv] b) I'm afraid of snakes.
[ə] c) Can I have a cup of coffee?

22. one [wʌn] a) He only needs one.
[wən] b) The green one'll do.

23. or [or] a) You can have ice cream or cake but not both.
[ər] b) There are one or two scoops in each dish.

24. that [ðæt] a) Is that the girl?
[ðət] b) She is the girl that I was telling you about.

25. the [ðiː] a) This is the book I've been looking for.
[ðə] b) Turn to the left.
[ði] c) It's on the edge.

26. to [tuː] a) Who did you speak to?
[tə] b) I spoke to Mr. Green.

27. was [wɑz] a) A: Is Susan here now?
B: Well, she was. Where did she go?
[wəz] b) She was just here.

28. would [wud] a) Would it be better to take a break?
[əd] b) What would happen to you?
[d] c) I'd be glad to.

29. who [huː] a) Who is she?
[hu] b) There's a girl who wants to see you.

Key Points 24

393-394

can と can't の発音

(1) 文中での can と can't の発音

例　A. I can take it. [ai kən teik it]
　　B. I can't take it. [ai kænt teik it]

日常会話のようなくだけた発話では，B は [kænt] の語尾の [t] が脱落して [ai kæn teik it] のような発音になることも多いので，聞き手は母音が [æ] か [ə] によって否定 (can't) か肯定 (can) かを判断しなくてはならない。[kæn] と [kən] では逆の意味になるので注意が必要である。

(2) 文尾にくる can と can't の発音

文尾にくる can や can't は強形で発音される。また肯定の can の [æn] は否定の can't の [ænt] より長く発音される。

例　Can I borrow your bicycle?
　　A. Yes, you can.
　　B. No, I'm afraid you can't.

また，can't はイギリス英語では [kænt] の代りに [kɑːnt] と発音されるので，肯定か否定かの区別は比較的容易である。

(3) 付加疑問文 can と can't の発音

付加疑問の can と can't は強形で発音される。

例　A. You can swim, can't you?
　　B. You can't play the guitar, can you?

can のほかに is, are, was, were, have, has, had なども文尾や付加疑問の場合には強形で発音される。

Key Points 25

395

that の強形と弱形

Ex.　A. This is the book that [ðət] I wanted to read.
　　B. I know that [ðət] she will come.
　　C. Look at that [ðæt] girl.
　　D. This is the reason for that [ðæt].

A，B の文中の that はそれぞれ関係代名詞と接続詞なので，弱形 [ðət] で発音される。しかし C, D の that はそれぞれ指示形容詞と指示代名詞であるので，強形 [ðæt] で発音される。

Exercise 27 396

Write the phonetic symbol [æ] or [ə] for the underlined vowels.

1. He says that she'll come if she can.
   [ ] [ ]
2. Here is the reason for that.
   [ ]
3. It's the best book that I've ever read.
   [ ]
4. I know that she'll come.
   [ ]
5. You haven't seen it, but I have.
   [ ] [ ]
6. You think that he can't do it, but I think he can.
   [ ] [ ] [ ]
7. I could have got up earlier if I'd had an alarm clock.
   [ ]
8. Who can play bass? Jenny can.
   [ ] [ ]
9. Do you know how much time we have?
   [ ]
10. What was that we heard?
   [ ]

Contraction (Contracted form)（縮約）

文の中で弱く読まれ，省略された単語を綴り字でも省略して書く場合があり，同じ弱形でも省略されて別の語と結合した場合を「縮約」と呼ぶ。この縮約という発音の仕方は，口語英語では普通に使われており，リズム感のある英語で話すには必要なことである。

A. be動詞 (am, are, is)の contraction 397

1. I'm (=I am) sorry.
2. You're (=you are) lucky.
3. He's (=he is) late.
4. It's (=it is) raining.
5. Who's (=who is) playing over there?
6. That girl's (=girl is) funny.

7. We're (=we are) students.
8. That's (=that is) interesting.
9. These're (=these are) different.
10. There's (=there is) some cake left in the fridge.

B. have動詞 (have, has, had)の contraction 398

1. I've (=I have) got to try again.
2. You've (=you have) been very kind.
3. He's (=he has) already left.
4. It's (=it has) been raining.
5. Mike's (=Mike has) been studying hard.
6. They've (=they have) finished their homework.
7. There's (=there has) been a campaign for the coming election.
8. We'd (=we had) been to the airport.
9. He'd (=he had) written all the postcards by noon.
10. You'd (=you had) better go to bed right now.

C. will, wouldの contraction 399

1. I'll (=I will) do it tomorrow.
2. He'll (=he will) be leaving soon.
3. I wonder if he'd (=he would) do it for us.
4. He asked me if you'd (=you would) come to the party.
5. I never expected she'd (=she would) recover so soon.
6. It'd (=it would) be my pleasure.

D. そのほか (us, not, etc.)の contraction 400

1. Let's (=let us) go, shall we?
2. That can't (=can not) be true!
3. Don't (=do not) cry, my dear.
4. Didn't you (=did you not) hear the news?
5. He oughtn't (=ought not) to drink so much.
6. Won't (=will not) you come in?
7. You shouldn't (=should not) smoke in bed.
8. You needn't (=need not) stay here.

Exercise 28 401

Listen to the audio and fill in the blanks.

1. Was he (   ) (   ) bus?
2. Did you ask (   ) (   )?
3. Give (   ) (   ) (   ).
4. I'm glad (   ) (   ) met you.
5. (   ) (   ) go.
6. (   ) (   ) leaving this afternoon.
7. (   ) like (   ) (   ) there?
8. I'd rather have this (   ) (   ).
9. What time is it? It's (   ) (   ) two.
10. He (   ) (   ) watching it.
11. Let's (   ) (   ) (   ) here.
12. (   ) (   ) (   ) you in a minute.
13. I (   ) (   ) about it.
14. (   ) (   ) me (   ) (   ) (   ) on.
15. I've (   ) (   ) it again (   ) again.
16. I (   ) put up (   ) (   ) any (   ).
17. It's supposed (   ) (   ) the best place (   ) (   ) (   ).

18. How ( ) the exam? O.K. I think I ( ) all right.

19. We ( ) ( ) put ( ) ( ) to this problem.

20. Swing it back ( ) forth.

21. He's ( ) make up ( ) ( ).

22. When I ( ) ( ) ( ), the line was busy.

23. He ( ) take part ( ) the contest.

24. Do you ( ) ( ) ( ) help ( ) ( )?

25. He said ( ) ( ) ( ) playing tennis.

26. I thought you ( ) ( ) ( ) it by now.

27. The ( ) already ( ).

28. ( ) ( ) ( ) ( ) studying English.

29. We ( ) ( ) all night.

30. He's ( ) ( ) lecturer to speak to his class.

31. There was a request ( ) ( ) ( ).

32. There was a request ( ) ( ) ( ) ( ).

33. That's the graduate student ( ) counselor is here.

34. That's the graduate student (　　　　　　) (　　　　　　) counselor here.

35. That's an (　　　　　　) fish.

36. That's an (　　　　　　) fish.

37. Her (　　　　　　) German.

38. Her (　　　　　　) German.

39. (　　　　　　) some old friends (　　　　　　) (　　　　　　).

40. (　　　　　　) some old friends (　　　　　　) (　　　　　　).

II INTONATION PATTERNS

音の高さ（pitch）には個人の声の高低による絶対的な高さと，発話の中で意味の違いを生ずる相対的な高さがある。イントネーション（音調）の高さはこの相対的で，普通下記のように四段に分けられる。

1.	/4/	最高	(extra high)	驚き，特別な強調等を表わす。
2.	/3/	高	(high)	
3.	/2/	中	(normal)	普通の高さ
4.	/1/	低	(low)	

イントネーションの表記には，いろいろな種類があるが，本書では次の音調曲線を用いる。

General Rules of Intonation Patterns

1 Falling intonation（下降調）↘ 402

(1) Declarative sentence（平叙文）

2 This is a 3 book. 1

2 I'd like an 3 apple. 1

(2) Imperative sentence（命令文）…上昇調を用いれば，「依頼」を表わすていねいな言い方になる。

Stand up.

Don't open the window.

(3) Wh- question（Wh 疑問文）

What did you ask?

Who is she?

How did you do it?

(4) Exclamatory sentence（感嘆文）

What a beautiful day!

How funny he is!

2 Rising intonation（上昇調）↗ 403

(1) General question (Yes/No question)（一般疑問文）

Are you ready?

Did you do it?

(2) Calling (Vocative)（呼びかけ）

Come here, Nancy.

Mother, where is my swimming suit?

(3) Repeated question（相手が言ったことをそのまま反復して問い返す場合）

A: We're all out of coffee.

B: Really? We're all out of coffee?

A: Who's coming tomorrow?

B: Who's coming tomorrow? Jane is.

その他：答えがよく聞き取れなかったため，反復して問い直す疑問文。

I beg your pardon? (= Excuse me, but what did you say?)

(cf. I beg your pardon. = I'm sorry, or Excuse me.)

3 Rising-falling intonation（上昇下降調）↗↘ 404

(1) Alternative question (Choice question, Or-question)（選択疑問文）

Closed choice（閉鎖的選択）↗↘ この場合は，否定疑問文で問うことはできない。

1. Would you like tea, or coffee? （紅茶とコーヒーのどちらがよろしいですか。）

Answers: I'd like tea, please.

I'd like coffee, please.

Nothing for me, thanks.

Neither thanks, but I could go for a glass of water.

2. Is her baby a boy or a girl?

3. Are you going there or not?

4. Did he buy a pen or a pencil?

(cf. Did you buy *a pen or pencil*?) ⤴

5. Which is larger, New York or Tokyo?

6. Who is taller, Jack or Paul?

参考 Open choice（開放的選択）⤴（これは上昇イントネーションのみ）

1. Would you like tea or coffee?（紅茶かコーヒーのような飲物はいかがですか。）

Answers: Yes, thanks. Tea, please. (Coffee, please.)

No, thank you. (Nothing to drink right now.)

2. Would you like apple pie or lemon pie? (or some other pies?)

3. Can she read or write?（彼女は読み書きができますか）

(cf. Is she reaing or writing?)

(2) Listing（列挙）⤴⤴⤴ …… ⤵

One, two, three, four, five.

She speaks English, German, French and Spanish.

4 Falling-rising/Fall-rise intonation（下降上昇調）⤵⤴ 405

I think we should start this project? (Uncertainty)

A: “So, you didn’t go to the store on Wednesday night?”

B: “Well ... I just don’t remember.” (Reluctant to reply)

I don't belong to any political party at the moment. (But my mind may change in future.)

Is this wallet yours? (Polite question)

Would you like some coffee? (Polite invitation)

5 Tag question（付加疑問文）↘ or ↗ 406

a) This is your book, isn't it? (Confirmation of the statement)

b) This is your book, isn't it? (Request for information)

a. I know this is your book. I am only asking you to confirm what I have said.
b. I really don't know whether this is your book or not. I'm asking you for information.

Exercise 29 407

Listen, compare a) and b) and answer.

1. a) Would you like some pie or ice cream? (I'd like pie.)

   b) Would you like some pie or ice cream? (Yes, please.)

2. a) Will you have some milk, or apple juice? (Neither thanks, but I could go for a glass of cold water.)

   b) Will you have some milk, or apple juice? (No, thank you.)

3. a) Would you like beer, sherry or gin? (Beer, please.)

   b) Would you like beer, sherry or gin? (Yes, thanks. Beer please.)

4. a) Could you come Sunday, or Monday? (Monday, early in the morning.)

   b) Could you come Sunday, or Monday? (Yes, early next week.)

5. a) Is he more or less happy? (He's happier than he's ever been.)

   b) Is he more or less happy? (Yes, I think he's reasonably well satisfied.)

Exercise 30 408

Listen, repeat and answer.

A. 1. Who is younger, Bill or Ted? (⤴⤵)

Bill (Ted) is.

2. Do you want bread or rice?

3. Was he happy or sad?

4. Do you prefer tomatoes, cucumbers or carrots?

5. Is he hungry or thirsty?

B. 1. Won't you have some cookies or some cakes? (⤴)

2. Could you come on Saturday or Sunday?

3. Have you been to London, or Paris or Rome?

4. Do you speak English, or French, or Italian?

5. Don't you play golf or tennis?

Exercise 31 409

Read the following questions and answer, using either (⤴⤵) or (⤴).

1. Which is taller, Mt. Fuji or Mt. Aso?
2. Did you stay home or go out?
3. Is the traffic light green, red or yellow?
4. Do you want to go now, later, or not at all?
5. Was he satisfied or unsatisfied?
6. Which would you rather have, roast beef or beef steak?
7. Did he go to Oxford or Cambridge?
8. Shall we go at ten or eleven?
9. Don't you have a motorbike or bicycle?
10. Does it come in a can or something?

Exercise 32 410

Listen to the following questions and repeat. Put either ⤴ or ⤵ at the end of each sentence.

1. a) You've been to New York, haven't you?

   b) You've been to New York, haven't you?

2. a) Jane can come, can't she?

   b) Jane can come, can't she?

3. a) You're not hungry, are you?

   b) You're not hungry, are you?

4. a) Polly wasn't wearing a raincoat, was she?

   b) Polly wasn't wearing a raincoat, was she?

Exercise 33 411

Make tag-questions and read the sentences aloud with the two different intonation patterns A and B.

A. Confirm the statement. B. Request for information.

1. He's your uncle.

   Ans. A. He's your uncle, isn't he? ⤵

   B. He's your uncle, isn't he? ⤴

2. She's your cousin.
3. Your brother's coming.
4. Her sisters are coming tomorrow.
5. That's your new dress.
6. Those flowers are dandelions.
7. You're pressed for time.
8. You know Carla Roberts.
9. His parents live in Chicago.
10. Your father speaks Spanish.

11. Jean enjoys ice skating.

12. You've been to San Francisco.

13. Nancy was here yesterday.

14. Mr. Green has already come.

15. You can swim.

16. John and Judy were in the same class last year.

17. You'll come along with us.

18. They'd rather stay at home this afternoon.

19. She'd already eaten.

20. We should study hard.

21. Your sister isn't coming.

22. Mr. Brown isn't your uncle.

23. Those birds aren't blackbirds.

24. They aren't coming together.

25. You don't live with your brother.

26. Your sister doesn't live with your parents.

27. You don't like snakes.

28. His mother doesn't speak Russian.

29. He isn't going to be elected.

30. You haven't met Uncle Jim.

31. Joan hasn't come yet.

32. He wasn't at home this afternoon.

33. Bill doesn't want the job.

34. You weren't in the same class last semester.

35. These children can't ski.

36. You won't go fishing tomorrow morning.

37. We shouldn't wait anymore.

38. There isn't a lot of fog here.

39. Today isn't Tuesday.

40. Your aunt wouldn't agree.

Exercise 34 412

Echo-question: Listen and repeat . Then tell the meaning of each dialog.

1. a) A: We don't have any butter.

B: Really? We don't have any butter?

b) A: You can have a day off tomorrow.

B: Really? I can have a day off tomorrow?

2. a) A: I'm reading a book.

B: What?

A: *Est of Eden.*

b) A: I'm reading a book.

B: What?

A: Well, I am, believe it or not.

c) A: I'm reading a book.

B: What?

A: I'm reading a book.

3. a) A: Martha has a new boyfriend.

B: Who?

A: George.

b) A: Martha has a new boyfriend.

B: Who?

A: Martha.

Exercise 35 413

Calling: Compare a) and b). Listen and repeat.

1. a) Can you hear, Jane?

   b) Can you hear Jane?

2. a) Who is it, Helen?

   b) Who is it? Helen?

3. a) How is your sister, Barbara?

   b) How is your sister Barbara?

4. a) Are you calling, Bob?

   b) Are you calling Bob?

5. a) Have you met, Mr. Thomas?

   b) Have you met Mr. Thomas?

6. a) Did you understand, Prof. Keene?

   b) Did you understand Prof. Keene?

7. a) I don't know, Ms. Johnson.

   b) I don't know Ms. Johnson.

8. a) We won't forget, Susan.

   b) We won't forget Susan.

Exercise 36 414

Make a question which might result in each of the following sentences (a.—d.).

Lucy was studying in her room last night.

a. ________________________________ . Lucy was.

b. ________________________________ . She was studying.

c. ________________________________ . She was studying in her room.

d. ________________________________ . She was studying last night.

Exercise 37 415

Listen and repeat. 音声を聞いてイントネーションの曲線をつけなさい。（同じ文を続けて書いてある箇所は，特にイントネーションによる文意やニュアンスの相違に注意。）

1. Are you ready?

2. Is she going to stay with us?

3. You know it as well as I do.

4. This car is more expensive than that one.

5. Yesterday's speech was better than today's.

6. Have you met my husband, Ms. Brown?
7. Margaret, I have something to tell you.
8. Ms. Thomas, this is Mr. Ford.
9. Mr. Newton, principal of our school, gave a very fine speech.
10. I saw Chris, Meg, and Karen.
11. This one is yellow; that one is green.
12. I don't want to go; it's too late.
13. By the way, where is Ms. Thompson?
14. If we miss the train, what shall we do?
15. He will tell you how important it is to be punctual.
16. It's incredible!
17. I never saw such a beautiful butterfly!
18. Don't worry!
19. May she rest in peace!
20. Do I know her? She is my mother!
21. A: Will you please bring it here?
    B: Mary will bring it to you.
22. What's she complaining about?
23. Open the window, will you please?
24. I thought she would go. (... but she didn't go.)
25. I thought she would go. (... and she did go.)
26. I think it's all right. (... less certainty)
27. I think it's all right. (... more certainty)

28. I think so. (... I'm not very sure.)

29. I think so. (... more certainty)

30. He didn't die, happily.

31. He didn't die happily.

32. The director says the actor's too old.

33. The director, says the actor, is too old.

34. The boys, I knew, were good.

35. The boys I knew were good.

36. Jennifer gave her dog biscuits. (Jennifer gave her dog biscuits to someone.)

37. Jennifer gave her dog biscuits. (Her dog was given biscuits by Jennifer.)

38. "Did you ask her to come?" said John.

39. John said, "Why did you ask him to come?"

40. It's time for the lesson to end.

41. It's time for the lesson to end?

42. A: Thank you.

    B: Thank you. (emphasis on 'you.')

43. A: Good-bye.

    B: Good-bye.

44. Mr. East gave a feast;
    Mr. North laid the cloth;
    Mr. West did his best.
    Mr. South burnt his mouth
    While eating a cold potato.

45. One, two, three, four, five,
Once I caught a fish alive.
Six, seven, eight, nine, ten,
Then I let him go again.

Why did you let it go?
Because it bit my finger so.
Which finger did it bite?
This little finger on the right.

主 要 参 考 文 献

安藤賢一 1984.『演習英語音声学』(*A Practical Course in English Phonetics*) 成美堂

Bowen, J. Donald. 1975. *Patterns of English Pronunciation, Massachusetts*. Newbury House Publishers. 河野守夫（訳）『口語米語の発音分析と演習』金星堂，1983.

Campbell, Peter D. 1983. *How the English Language is Pronounced*. ELE

Celce-Murcia, M., Brinton, D. M., & Goodwin, J. M. 2010. *Teaching Pronunciation: A Course Book and Reference Guide*. New York: Cambridge University Press.

出口保夫（編著）1978.『マザー・グースのうた』評論社

藤井健三 1986.『現代英語発音の基礎——日英音声比較』研究社

藤野紀男 1984.『マザー・グースの唄が聞こえる』朝日イブニングニュース社

Gimson, A.C. 1983[3]. *An Introduction to the Pronunciation of English*. London: Edward Arnold.

竹林 滋（訳）『英語音声学入門』金星堂，1984.

郡司利男（編著）1983.『英語学習逆引辞典』開文社

服部四郎 1984.『音声学』岩波書店

平野敬一（編）1973.『マザー・グース童謡集』ELEC 出版部

平野敬一（編）1977.『続・マザー・グース童謡集』ELEC 出版部

一色マサ子・松井千枝 1978.『英語音声学：日本語との比較による』朝日出版社

Jones, Daniel. 1975[9]. *An Outline of English Phonetics,* Cambridge : Cambridge University Press.

梶井弥寿子 1978.『アメリカ英語の発音とイントネーション——最新米語発音教本』(*Pronunciation and Intonation of American English*) I.T.S. インターナショナル・テキストブックサービス

Kenyon, J. S., & Knott, T. A. 1953. *A Pronouncing Dictionary of American English*. Springfield, Massachusetts: G. & C. Merriam Company, Publishers

高本捨三郎 1969. *New English Phonology: A Contrastive Study of English and Japanese Pronunciation*. 南雲堂

Ladefoged, P., & Johnson, K. 2015. *A Course in Phonetics* (7th ed.). Stamford: Cengage Learning.

高本捨三郎（絹著）1984.『英語の発音とヒアリング』(*Aural-Oral Approach to Modern English*) 南雲堂

木村恒夫 1963.『英語発音の基礎』(*Improve Your English Pronunciation*) 開拓社

木村恒夫 1968.『英語発音学演習』(*A Shorter Course in American English Pronunciation*) 開拓社

Lehiste, Ilse. 1969. *Suprasegmentals*. Cambridge, Massachusetts, and London, England: The M.I.T. Press.

牧野 勤 1977.『英語発音——指導と学習——』東京書籍

牧野 勤・谷美奈子・斉藤勉 1978.『新・英語音声学教本』愛育社

Mackenzie, M.D. Munro. 1967. *Modern English Pronunciation Practice*. Longman.

枡矢好弘 1976.『英語音声学』(English Phonetics) こびあん書房

松居 司・ポール・スノードン 1979.『英語の発音——基礎編』(*Pronunciation Practice in English First Level*) 開拓社

ミシガン大学英語研究所（編）1958.『英語の発音』(*English Pronunciation*) 黒田巍（訳）大修館

Milne, B. Lumsden. 1951. *Modern Speech Training*, London : Macmillan, 松野和彦（編訳）『英語発音演習』英宝社，1977.

三宅川正・増山節夫 1971.『最新英語音声学教本』(*A New Course in English Phonetics*) 英宝社

三宅川正・増山節夫 1987.『英語音声学——理論と実際——』(*English Phonetics : Theoretical and Practical*) 英宝社

Mortimer, Colin. 1985. *Elements of Pronunciation, London*. Cambridge University Press.

中島文雄・他 1965.『（テープによる）アメリカ英語の発音教本』(*American English — A Drill Book*) 研究社

根間弘海 1986.『英語の発音演習』大修館

日本音声学会（編）1976.『音声学大辞典』(*A Dictionary of Phonetics*) 三修社

Nilsen, Don L.F., & Nilsen Alleen P. 1971. *Pronunciation Contrasts in English*. New York: Regents Publishing Company.

西出公之・他（編著）1984.『英語発音の基礎演習』(*Basic Practice in English Pronunciation*) 三修社

O'Connor, J.D. 1980. *Better English Pronunciation* (New Edition). Cambridge: Cambridge University Press.

小川芳男 1955.『図解・英語小発音学』有精堂出版

小栗敬三 1966.『英語音声学概論』(*English Phonetics*) 篠崎書林

小栗敬三 1966.『英語発音の知識』(*English Pronunciation*) 篠崎書林

小栗敬三 1983.『英語音声学』(*English Phonetics*) 篠崎書林

奥田夏子 1975.『英語のイントネーション——研究と指導——』英和出版

大西雅行・都築正喜 1977.『英語音声学入門』学書房

太田 朗 1959.『米語音素論』研究社

Pike, K.L. 1945. *The Intonation of American English. Ann Arbor*: University of Michigan Press.

Prator, C.H. Jr., & B.W. Robinett. 1972[3]. *Manual of American English Pronunciation*. New York : Holt, Ringehart and Winston. 大浦幸男・鴫原真一（訳）『アメリカ英語発音教本』英潮社新社，1969.

佐藤寧・佐藤努 1997.『現代の英語音声学』金星堂

Scott, Charles T. 1974. *English Pronunciation and Intonation*. Tokyo: ELEC

ロベルジュ・クロード・霜崎 實・許圭 南 1985.『VT 法による英語発音指導教本』研究社

関根応之 1987.『5 分間英語発音』(*A Shorter Course in American & British English Pronunciation*) 南雲堂

島岡 丘 1978.『現代英語の音声』(*Mastering the Sound of English*) 研究社

島岡 丘 1986.『教室の英語音声学』研究社

島岡 丘・佐藤寧 1987.『最新の音声学・音韻論——現代英語を中心に』研究社

竹中治郎 1955.『簡約英詩法と鑑賞法』(*Concise English Prosody and Poetry Appreciation*) 篠崎書林

竹中治郎 1957.『英語発音セミナー』(*Phonetic Transcriptions & Readings in English*) 泰文堂
竹林 滋 1982.『英語音声学入門』大修館
竹内真生子 2012.『［DVD&CD 付］日本人のための英語発音完全教本』アスク出版
鳥居次好・兼子尚道 1962.『英語の発音：研究と指導』大修館
鳥居次好・兼子尚道 1969.『英語発音の指導』大修館
Trager, G.L., & H.L. Smith, Jr. 1957^{3}. *An Outline of English Structure*. Washington, D.C.: *American Council of Learned Societies*. 太田 朗（訳）『英語構造の概要』大修館，1968.
有働眞理子・谷明信（編著）2018.『英語音声教育実践と音声学・音韻論　効果的で豊かな発音の学びを目指して』ジアース教育新社
渡辺和幸 1987.『コミュニケーションのための英語音声学』(*English Phonetics for Communication*) 弓書房
山見由紀子・赤塚麻里・久保田一充 2017.『子どもとはじめる英語発音とフォニックス』南雲堂
山本まつよ・百々佑利子 1983.『詩とナーサリーライム第 1 集』(*Poems & Nursery Rhymes 1*)（株）テック・ラボ教育センター
山本まつよ・百々佑利子 1985.『詩とナーサリーライム第 2 集』(*Poems & Nursery Rhymes 2*)（株）テック・ラボ教育センター
米山明日香 2021.『英語「発音記号」の鬼 50 講』明日香出版社
The English Journal（別冊）ゼロからスタート！ 英語ヒアリング特訓本 1985. 2. アルク
The English Journal 13（別冊）やさしい日常会話のヒアリング 1986. 2. アルク

FAIRY TALES
COSMOS
encyclopedia
POEMS
dino
ABC
1 2
BIRDS
princess
ATLAS
ADVENTURE

English Pronunciation for Communication <Revised Edition>
コミュニケーションへの英語発音演習【改訂新版】 [B-970]

1　刷　2024年3月19日

編著者	杉森　直樹	Naoki Sugimori
著　者	小泉　節子	Setsuko Koizumi
	杉森　幹彦	Mikihiko Sugimori
発行者	南雲　一範　Kazunori Nagumo	
発行所	株式会社　南雲堂	
	〒162-0801　東京都新宿区山吹町361	
	NAN'UN-DO Co., Ltd.	
	361 Yamabuki-cho, Shinjuku-ku, Tokyo 162-0801, Japan	
	振替口座 : 00160-0-46863	
	TEL: 03-3268-2311（代表）／FAX: 03-3269-2486	
	編集者　加藤　敦	
組　版	中西　史子	
装　丁	銀月堂	
検　印	省　略	
コード	ISBN978-4-523-17970-2　C0082	

Printed in Japan

E-mail　nanundo@post.email.ne.jp
URL　https://www.nanun-do.co.jp/